CHAPMAN
NAVIGATION
RULES

CHAPMAN'S GUIDE TO THE RULES OF THE ROAD

CHAPMAN
NAVIGATION RULES

U.S. DEPARTMENT OF HOMELAND SECURITY
UNITED STATES COAST GUARD

INTERNATIONAL—INLAND
NAVIGATION RULES COMDTINST M16672.2D

HEARST BOOKS
A DIVISION OF STERLING PUBLISHING CO., INC.
NEW YORK

Auxiliary text and art copyright © 2004 Hearst Communications, Inc.
All rights reserved.

Book Design by Renato Stanisic Design
Cover Design by Celia Fuller
Copy Edited by Kris Christian

Library of Congress Cataloging-in-Publication Data.
United States. Coast Guard.
  Chapman navigation rules / United States Coast Guard & Dan Fales.
      p. cm.
  ISBN 1-58816-325-3
  1. Inland navigation--Law and legislation--United States. 2. Navigation--Safety regulations--United States. 3. Rule of the road at sea. I. Fales, Dan. II. Title.
  KF2566.A33 2004
  343.7309'66--dc22

                                                    2004000443

10 9 8 7 6 5 4 3 2 1

Published by Hearst Books
A Division of Sterling Publishing Co., Inc.
387 Park Avenue South, New York, N.Y. 10016

Includes complete text of United States Coast Guard, Navigation Rules: International– Inland (Nov 29, 2003 edition); published by the Government Printing Office.

CHAPMAN and CHAPMAN PILOTING and Hearst Books are trademarks owned by Hearst Communications, Inc.

Distributed in Canada by Sterling Publishing
c/o Canadian Manda Group, One Atlantic Avenue, Suite 105
Toronto, Ontario, Canada M6K 3E7

Printed in China

ISBN 1-58816-325-3

CHANGES TO THE RULES

The Rules as presented here reflect all the changes made up to April 25, 2003, with reference to those additions to the International Rules effective on November 29, 2003. But from time to time other changes will be made in the Rules. This information and other data is available on the U.S. Coast Guard's Navigation Center web site at www.navcen.uscg.gov

More detailed changes are at
www.navcen.uscg.gov/mwv/navrules/changes.htm

To download a copy of the actual Rules go to
www.navcen.uscg.gov/mwv/navrules/rotr_online.htm

CONTENTS

RULE 24. Towing and pushing   60

(a) Power-driven vessels when towing astern.

(b) Pushing vessel and pushed vessel rigidly connected in composite unit.

(c) Power-driven vessel when pushing ahead or towing alongside.

(d) Compliance with other requirements.

(e) Vessels being towed.

(f) Vessels being towed alongside or pushed in a group.

(g) Inconspicuous, partly submerged vessel or object being towed.

(h) Alternative lighting of vessel or object being towed.

(i) Western Rivers or other specified waters; exception.

(j) Towing another vessel in distress or otherwise in need of assistance.

RULE 25. Sailing vessels underway and vessels under oars   68

(a) Sailing vessels underway.

(b) Sailing vessels of less than 20 meters **(65.6 ft.)** in length.

(c) Additional lights.

(d) Sailing vessels of less than 7 meters **(23 ft.)** in length; vessels under oars.

(e) Vessels proceeding under sail and propelled by machinery.

RULE 26. Fishing vessels   70

(a) Exhibition of only prescribed lights and shapes.

(b) Vessels engaged in trawling.

(c) Vessels engaged in fishing other than trawling.

(d) Vessels engaged in fishing in close proximity to other vessels engaged in fishing.

(e) Vessels when not engaged in fishing.

RULE 27. Vessels not under command or restricted in their ability to maneuver   72

(a) Vessels not under command.

(b) Vessels restricted in their ability to maneuver.

(c) Vessels engaged in towing operations.

(d) Vessels engaged in dredging or underwater operations.

(e) Vessels engaged in diving operations.

(f) Vessels engaged in mineclearance operations.

(g) Vessels of less than 12 meters **(39.4 ft.)** in length.

(h) Signals of vessels in distress and requiring assistance.

(a) Vessels engaged on pilotage duty.

(b) Vessels when not engaged on pilotage duty.

(a) Vessels at anchor.

(b) Vessels of less than 50 meters **(164 ft.)** in length; alternative light.

(c) Illumination of decks.

(d) Vessels aground.

(e) Vessels of less than 7 meters **(23 ft.)** in length when at anchor.

(f) Vessels of less than 12 meters **(39.4 ft.)** in length when aground.

(g) Vessels of less than 20 meters **(65.6 ft.)** in length while at anchor in special anchorage.

PART D, SOUND AND LIGHT SIGNALS

(a) Vessels of 12 meters **(39.4 ft.)** or more in length.

(b) Vessels of less than 12 meters **(39.4 ft.)** in length.

(a) Whistle signals.

(b) Light signals.

(c) Overtaking situations.

(d) Doubts or failure to understand signals.

(e) Vessels in areas of obscured visibility due to intervening obstructions.

(f) Use of one whistle only on a vessel.

(g) Power-driven vessels leaving dock or berth.

(h) Agreement between vessels using radiotelephone.

(a) Power-driven vessels making way through the water.

(b) Power-driven vessels underway but stopped and making no way through the water.

(c) Vessels not under command; vessels restricted in ability to maneuver; sailing vessels; vessels engaged in fishing; vessels engaged in towing or pushing.

(d) Vessels towed.

(e) Pushing and pushed vessels connected in composite unit.

(f) Vessels at anchor.

(g) Vessels aground.

(h) Vessels of less than 12 meters **(39.4 ft.)** in length.

(i) Pilot vessels.

(j) Vessels anchored in special anchorage areas.

HOW TO USE THIS BOOK

These Rules are written not to guarantee privilege or rights-of-way but to prevent collisions of vessels operating in both offshore and inshore waters. There are correspondingly two sets of Rules: International and Inland. The International Rules are known as the 72 COLREGS because they were formulated during the 1972 Convention on the International Regulations for Preventing Collisions of Vessels at Sea. They apply to those waters seaward of the demarcation lines as established by regulations starting on page 22. The Inland Navigation Rules apply on waters inshore of those lines.

Both sets of Rules are organized into five parts covering General applications, Steering and Sailing, Lights and Shapes, Sound and Light Signals, and, finally, Exemptions. Generally, the International and Inland Rules are exactly the same. But where they differ, a change to *italic* **type** will be noted. An abbreviation, either **INTL** or **INLD** in **red type**, will indicate that the change belongs to the International or Inland Rules. At those Rules of particular interest to recreational boaters, comments will be made in **blue type**.

Although all the Rules apply to the operators of pleasure boats, some Rules are of more significance than others. The actual Rules come from the U.S. Coast Guard. The **Comments** are inserted by the editors only as aids to understanding.

Remember, the Rules as they appear here and the **Comments** with them are not of a legal nature. For the actual legal foundations, refer to Legal Citations on page 164.

The International and Inland Rules are very similar in their wording and application. For most Rules there is no difference. Therefore in this book we have combined the International and Inland Navigation Rules so comparison between the two is easier. All efforts have been made to ensure these Navigation Rules are complete and accurate; however, the U.S. Coast Guard and the publisher make no claims, promises, or guarantees about the accuracy, completeness, or adequacy of the contents and expressly disclaim liability for errors and omissions. Because of formatting changes, consider these Rules an informational version and as such should NOT be used as evidence in legal proceedings. Those seeking official versions of the Navigation Rules should refer to the International Navigational Rules Act of 1977 (Public Law 95-75, 91 Stat. 308, or 33 U.S.C. 1601-1608), and the Inland Navigation Rules Act of 1980 (Public Law 96-591, 94 Stat. 3415, 33 U.S.C. 2001-2038).

While reading the Navigation Rules, you should be aware of some formatting and layout conventions. If a paragraph or word is *italicized*, that means there is no corresponding paragraph or word in the other set of Rules. The set of Rules the paragraph or word applies to will be at the end of the italicized text and look like this: **INTL** or **INLD**:

> (e) A vessel proceeding under sail when also being propelled by machinery shall exhibit forward where it can best be seen a conical shape, apex downwards. *A vessel of less than 12 meters in length is not required to exhibit this shape, but may do so.* **INLD**

If the paragraph numbering differs between International and Inland Rules of a similar topic, the numbering will look like this: (d/f). In all cases, the International Rule numbering will be on the left and the Inland Rule numbering will be on the right.

If the International and Inland Rules are significantly different, such that the section must be viewed as separate paragraphs, the Rule will look like this:

(i) a vessel intending to overtake another shall in compliance with Rule 9(e)(i) indicate her intention by the following signals on her whistle: - two prolonged blasts followed by one short blast to mean "I intend to overtake you on your starboard side"	(i) a power-driven vessel intending to overtake another power-driven vessel shall indicate her intention by the following signals on her whistle:- one short blast to mean "I intend to overtake you on your starboard side"

In all cases, the International Rule will be on the left and the Inland Rule will be on the right.

Minor differences between Rules will be delineated within the text next to each other. In all cases, the International Rule will be on the left and the Inland Rule will be on the right. For example, if the bulk of the text was the same between a particular International and Inland Rule, but referenced another Rule differently, the paragraph would look something like this:

(c) Every vessel shall have due regard to the prevailing circumstances and conditions of restricted visibility when complying with **[the Rules of Section I of this Part / Rules 4 through 10]**.

Insignificant differences between sets of Rules, such as "1" vs. "one" or missing words that don't change the meaning of a Rule, will not be identified. At times captions on illustrations may be duplicated and confusing. The Rule numbers and the following letters are often the same. This is because multiple illustrations may be used to explain a single subparagraph in a particular Rule.

Rule 24a is one example where two illustrations have the same letters. In Rule24f four drawings are similarly identified.

The International Navigation Rules **do not** confer upon any vessel the "right of way"; however, certain vessels "in sight of each other" are responsible "to keep out of the way" of others. Usually, power-driven vessels are to keep out of the way of a vessel "not under command or restricted in her ability to maneuver", sailing vessels or a "vessel engaged in fishing". However, some exceptions exist when they themselves are "not in command" or "restricted in her ability to maneuver" (Rule 18), are overtaking another vessel (Rule 13), are navigating a "narrow channel or fairway" (Rule 9), and in other less explicit circumstances.

Navigation Rules should be regarded as a "code of conduct" and not a "bill of rights". They do not bestow rights or privileges, but impose the duty to either "give-way" or "stand-on", dependent on the circumstances. What is important is not so much what things are, but how to avoid collisions. Understand, the Rules are in place to "prevent collisions", not to define nautical terms or to be subjected to strict interpretation.

Finally, having said all this, the ordinary practice of seamen requires precaution under all conditions and circumstances and not strict adherence to the Rules or any other practice. Although strict adherence may not always be prudent, the Rules are very precise in stating that *nothing* "shall exonerate any vessel, or the owner, master or crew thereof, from the consequences of any neglect" (Rule 2). Neglect, among other things, could be not maintaining a proper look-out (Rule 5), use of improper speed (Rule 6), not taking the appropriate actions to determine and avoid collision (Rules 7 and 8), or completely ignoring your responsibilities under the Rules—The Editors.

HISTORY

Today's International and Inland Rules, while similar in wording, come from different backgrounds and apply to different waters. Both, however, are dedicated to the same aim: the prevention of collisions between vessels—commercial, governmental and recreational as well. Here's some background.

INTERNATIONAL RULES

The International Rules in this book were formalized in the Convention on the International Regulations for Preventing Collisions at Sea, 1972, and became effective on July 15, 1977. The Rules (commonly called 72 COLREGS) are part of the Convention, and vessels flying the flags of states ratifying the treaty are bound to the Rules. The United States has ratified this treaty and all United States flag vessels must adhere to these Rules where applicable. President Gerald R. Ford proclaimed 72 COLREGS and the Congress adopted them as the International Navigational Rules Act of 1977.

The 72 COLREGS were developed by the Inter-Governmental Maritime Consultative Organization (IMCO) which in May 1982 was renamed the International Maritime Organization (IMO). In November 1981, IMO's Assembly adopted 55 amendments to the 72 COLREGS which became effective on June 1, 1983. The IMO also adopted 9 more amendments which became effective on November 19, 1989, **and an additional 9 effective on November 29, 2003.**

The International Rules in this book contain these amendments. These Rules are applicable on waters outside of established navigational lines of demarcation. The lines are called COLREGS Demarcation Lines and delineate those waters upon which mariners shall comply with the Inland and International Rules. COLREGS Demarcation Lines are contained in this book.

INLAND RULES

The Inland Rules in this book replace the old Inland Rules, Western Rivers Rules, Great Lakes Rules, their respective pilot rules and interpretive rules, and parts of the Motorboat Act of 1940. Many of the old navigation rules were originally enacted in the last century. Occasionally, provisions were added to cope with the increasing complexities of water transportation. Eventually, the navigation rules for United States inland waterways became such a confusing patchwork of requirements that in the 1960's several attempts were made to revise and simplify them. These attempts were not successful.

Following the signing of the Convention on the International Regulations for Preventing Collisions at Sea, 1972, a new effort was made to unify and update the various inland navigation rules. This effort culminated in the enactment of the Inland Navigational Rules Act of 1980. This legislation sets out Rules 1 through 38— the main body of the Rules. The five Annexes were published as regulations.

It is important to note that with the exception of Annex V to the Inland Rules, the International and Inland Rules and Annexes are very similar in both content and format.

The effective date for the Inland Navigation Rules was December 24, 1981, except for the Great Lakes where the effective date was March 1, 1983.

NAVIGATION RULES INTERNATIONAL—INLAND

These Rules are designed to prevent collisions of vessels operating in both International and Inland waters. The International Rules, known as the COLREGS, apply to those waters seaward of the demarcation lines as established by regulations starting on page 22. Inland Rules apply on waters inshore of those lines.

The Rules are organized into five parts covering General applications, Steering and Sailing, Lights and Shapes, Sound and Light Signals, and, finally, Exemptions. Generally, the International and Inland Rules are exactly the same. But where they differ, a change to *italic type* will be noted. An abbreviation, either **INTL** or **INLD** in **red type**, will indicate that the change belongs to a specific set of Rules.

COMMENTS will be made in **blue type** at those Rules of particular interest to recreational boaters. Although all the Rules apply to the operators of pleasure boats, some Rules are of more significance than others. The actual Rules come from the U.S. Coast Guard. The Comments are inserted by the editors only as aids to understanding.

Remember, the Rules as they appear here and the Comments with them are not of a legal nature. For the actual legal foundations refer to Legal Citations on page 164—The Editors.

PART A, GENERAL RULES
RULES 1-3

Rules 1, 2, and 3 make up the general opening to both the International and Inland Navigation Rules. While Rule 3 defines many of the terms used, Rule 2 actually details the responsibilities shouldered by those who operate any vessel including recreational boats of any size, power, rigging, and description—The Editors.

RULE 1. INTERNATIONAL

(a) These Rules shall apply to all vessels upon the high seas and in all waters connected therewith navigable by seagoing vessels.

(b) Nothing in these Rules shall interfere with the operation of special rules made by an appropriate authority for roadsteads, harbors, rivers, lakes, or inland waterways connected with the high seas and navigable by seagoing vessels. Such special rules shall conform as closely as possible to these Rules.

(c) Nothing in these Rules shall interfere with the operation of any special rules made by the Government of any State with respect to additional station or signal lights, shapes or whistle signals for ships of war and vessels proceeding under convoy, with respect to additional station or signal lights or shapes for fishing vessels engaged in fishing as a fleet. These additional station or signal lights, shapes or whistle signals shall, so far as possible, be such that they cannot be mistaken for any light, shape, or signal authorized elsewhere under these Rules.[1] **[See Rule 23(b)]**

1 Submarines may display, as a distinctive means of identification, an intermittent flashing amber (yellow) beacon with a sequence of operation of one flash per second for three (3) seconds followed by a three (3) second off-period. Other special rules made by the Secretary of the Navy with respect to additional station and signal lights are found in Part 706 of Title 32, Code of Federal Regulations (32 CFR 706).

(d)   Traffic separation schemes may be adopted by the Organization for the purpose of these Rules.
        (See Rule 10)

(e)   Whenever the Government concerned shall have determined that a vessel of special construction or purpose cannot comply fully with the provisions of any of these Rules with respect to number, position, range or arc of visibility of lights or shapes, as well as to the disposition and characteristics of sound-signaling appliances, such vessel shall comply with such other provisions in regard to number, position, range or arc of visibility of lights or shapes, as well as to the disposition and characteristics of sound-signaling appliances, as her Government shall have determined to be the closest possible compliance with these Rules in respect to that vessel.

(a)   These Rules apply to all vessels upon the inland waters of the United States, and to vessels of the United States on the Canadian waters of the Great Lakes to the extent that there is no conflict with Canadian law.

(b)   (i)   These Rules constitute special rules made by an appropriate authority within the meaning of Rule 1(b) of the International Regulations.

        (ii) All vessels complying with the construction and equipment requirements of the International Regulations are considered to be in compliance with these Rules.

(c)   Nothing in these Rules shall interfere with the operation of any special rules made by the Secretary of the Navy with respect to additional station or signal lights and shapes or whistle signals for ships of war and vessels proceeding under convoy, or by the Secretary with respect to additional station or signal lights and shapes for fishing vessels engaged in fishing as a fleet. These additional station or signal lights and shapes or whistle signals shall, so far as possible, be such that they cannot be mistaken for any light, shape or signal authorized elsewhere under these Rules. Notice of such special rules shall be published in the Federal Register and, after the effective date specified in such notice, they shall have effect as if they were a part of these Rules.[1] **[See Rule 23(b)]**

This is the umbrella that subjects all vessels as defined in Rule 3(a), be they power-driven or not, to the Inland Navigation Rules. By the way, such vessels include personal watercraft and small inflatables.

Inland waters as defined in Rule 3(o) are those navigable waters inshore or shoreside of the 72 COLREGS lines that separate International from Inland waters. On the navigation charts the COLREGS lines are magenta in color and generally are drawn from headland to headland, across the mouths of harbors and across entrances to inlets. For more details see the section on COLREGS Demarcation Lines starting on page 125. Though Inland waters include the Great

Lakes, they do not include those freshwater impoundments wholly contained within a state. Here state laws apply.
Rule 1(b) allows the United States to set up its own Rules in Inland waters. Generally these mirror the International Rules except in some areas like those found in Rule 34, where Inland differs from International—The Editors.

(d)   Traffic separation schemes may be established for the purposes of these Rules. Vessel traffic service regulation may be in effect in certain areas.

Magenta zones separate charted locations of inbound and outbound vessel traffic lanes at major ports. Vessels under 65.6 ft. (20 meters) and all sailing vessels, including recreational boats, are prohibited from impeding the progress of those vessels required to use the lanes. [Rule 10(j)]

(e)   Whenever the Secretary determines that a vessel or class of vessels of special construction or purpose cannot comply fully with the provisions of any of these Rules with respect to the number, position, range, or arc of visibility of lights or shapes, as well as to the disposition and characteristics of sound-signaling appliances, the vessel shall comply with such other provisions in regard to the number, position, range, or arc of visibility of lights or shapes, as well as to the disposition and characteristics of sound-signaling appliances, as the Secretary shall have determined to be the closest possible compliance with these Rules. The

Secretary may issue a certificate of alternative compliance for a vessel or class of vessels specifying the closest possible compliance with these Rules. The Secretary of the Navy shall make these determinations and issue certificates of alternative compliance for vessels of the Navy.

(f) The Secretary may accept a certificate of alternative compliance issued by a contracting party to the International Regulations if he determines that the alternative compliance standards of the contracting party are substantially the same as those of the United States.

RULE 2. RESPONSIBILTY

(a) Nothing in these Rules shall exonerate any vessel, or the owner, master, or crew thereof, from the consequences of any neglect to comply with these Rules or of the neglect of any precaution which may be required by the ordinary practice of seamen, or by the special circumstances of the case.

(b) In construing and complying with these Rules due regard shall be had to all dangers of navigation and collision and to any special circumstances, including the limitations of the vessels involved, which may make a departure from these Rules necessary to avoid immediate danger.

For all mariners, most especially recreational boaters, Rule 2(a) lays out a skipper's responsibility to follow the Rules and when necessary [2(b)] depart from them. For example, in a crossing situation with power-driven vessels within sight of one another, the vessel required to maintain course and speed [Rule 17(a)(i)] could deviate from that Rule should it be obvious that his failure to do so would result in a collision. You also don't want to neglect the Rules, such as failing to sound the appropriate signals when operating in fog—The Editors.

For the purpose of these Rules *and this Chapter* **INLD**, except where the context otherwise requires:

(a)   The word "vessel" includes every description of watercraft, including non-displacement craft, *WIG craft* **INTL** (effective 11/29/03) and seaplanes, used or capable of being used as a means of transportation on water.

On November 29, 2003 a number of additions were made to the International Rules but not the Inland Rules. For the most part these additions involved WIGs (Wing-In-Ground) craft—The Editors.

A WIG is a combination air-cushion craft, airboat and seaplane. It can be a single seater or a multi-passenger model. See subparagraph (m).

(b)   The term "power-driven vessel" means any vessel propelled by machinery.

(c)   The term "sailing vessel" means any vessel under sail provided that propelling machinery, if fitted, is not being used.

(d) The term "vessel engaged in fishing" means any vessel fishing with nets, lines, trawls, or other fishing apparatus which restrict maneuverability, but does not include a vessel fishing with trolling lines or other fishing apparatus which do not restrict manageability.

Many sportfishermen erroneously believe they fall into this category when trolling lines. Under this definition, they do not. This becomes important when Rule 18 is applied where a vessel engaged in fishing (trawling not trolling) can claim some right-of-way privileges. Sportfishermen sometimes do when they shouldn't. However, giving a wide berth to a trolling sportfisherman with lines set astern can be considered a courtesy—The Editors.

(e) The term "seaplane" includes any aircraft designed to maneuver on the water.

(f) The term "vessel not under command" means a vessel which through some exceptional circumstance is unable to maneuver as required by these Rules and is therefore unable to keep   out of the way of another vessel.

(g) The term "vessel restricted in her ability to maneuver" means a vessel which from the nature of her work is restricted in her ability to maneuver as required by these Rules and is therefore unable to keep out of the way of another vessel. *The term* **INTL** "vessels restricted in their ability to maneuver" *shall* **INTL** include but not be limited to:

(i) A vessel engaged in laying, servicing, or picking up a navigational mark, submarine cable or pipeline;

(ii) A vessel engaged in dredging, surveying or underwater operations;

(iii) A vessel engaged in replenishment or transferring persons, provisions or cargo while underway;

(iv) A vessel engaged in the launching or recovery of air craft;

(v) A vessel engaged in mine clearance operations;

(vi) A vessel engaged in a towing operation such as severly restricts the towing vessel and her tow in their ability to deviate from their course.

(h) *The term "vessel constrained by her draft" means a power-driven vessel which because of her draft in relation to the available depth and width of navigable water is severely restricted in her ability to deviate from the course she is following.* **INTL**

Note that a COD (vessel contained by draft) is not provided similar status under the Inland Rules—The Editors.

(i/h) The word "underway" means that a vessel is not at anchor, or made fast to the shore, or aground.

It's important to understand this definition because "underway" is used in both state and federal regulations, especially those involving the wearing of life preservers. A vessel does not actually have to be moving through the water either under engine or sail power to be underway. A vessel drifting or simply stopped in open water is actually underway—The Editors.

(j/i) length overall and greatest breadth.

(k/j) Vessels shall be deemed to be in sight of one another only when one can be observed visually from the other.

(l/k) The term "restricted visibility" means any condition in which visibility is restricted by fog, mist, falling snow, heavy rainstorms, sandstorms, or any other similar causes.

(m) *The term "Wing-In-Ground (WIG) craft" means a multimodal craft which, in its main operational mode, flies in close proximity to the surface by utilizing surface-effect action.* **INTL** (effective 11/29/03)

Waters beyond the breakwater are governed by the International rules. The Inland rules apply to the waters in shore of the breakwater. Note the magenta COLREGS Demaracation Line

(l)   *"Western Rivers" means the Mississippi River, its tributaries, South Pass, and Southwest Pass, to the navigational demarcation lines dividing the high seas from harbors, rivers and other inland waters of the United States, and the Port Allen-Morgan City Alternate Route, and that part of the Atchafalaya River above its junction with the Port Allen-Morgan City Alternate Route including the Old River and the Red River;* **INLD**

(m)   *"Great Lakes" means the Great Lakes and their connecting tributary waters including the Calumet River as far as the Thomas J. O'Brien Lock and Controlling Waters (between mile 326 and 327), the Chicago River as far as the east side of the Ashland Avenue Bridge (between mile 321 and 322), and the Saint Lawrence River as far east as the lower exit of Saint Lambert Lock;* **INLD**

(n)   *"Secretary" means the Secretary of the department in which the Coast Guard is operating;* **INLD**

(o)   *"Inland Waters" means the navigable waters of the United States shoreward of the navigational demarcation lines dividing the high seas from harbors, rivers and other inland waters of the United States and the waters of the Great Lakes on the United States side of the International Boundary;* **INLD**

(p)   *"Inland Rules" or "Rules" mean the Inland Navigational Rules and the annexes thereto, which govern the conduct of vessels and specify the lights, shapes, and sound signals that apply on inland waters; and* **INLD**

(q)   *"International Regulations" means the International Regulations for Preventing Collisions at Sea, 1972, including annexes currently in force for the United States.* **INLD**

PART B, STEERING AND SAILING RULES
SECTION I / SUBPART I
CONDUCT OF VESSELS IN ANY CONDITION OF VISIBILITY
Rules 4-10

RULE 4/5. APPLICATION / LOOKOUT

Rules in this section apply to any condition of visibility.

Rules 4 through 19 make up the STEERING AND SAILING RULES. This is PART B of the Rules which in turn consist of three divisions: "Conduct of Vessels in any Condition of Visibility (Rules 4–10)," "Conduct of Vessels in Sight of One Another (Rules 11-18)," and "Conduct of Vessels in Restricted Visibility (Rule 19)." In the International version these divisions are called Section I, II, & III; in the Inland Rules, Subpart I, II, & III. These Rules lay out the responsibilities assigned to all vessels regardless of visibility, such as maintaining a proper lookout, defining safe speed, and avoiding the risk of collision. They also establish the rights-of-way priorities when vessels are within sight of each other (Rules 11-18); and in Rule 19 set out the actions to be taken when operating under conditions of restricted visibility such as fog, rain, snow, or the like. Rule 19 also calls upon skippers to use radar when underway in limited visibility—The Editors.

RULE 5

Every vessel shall at all times maintain a proper look-out by sight and hearing as well as by all available means appropriate in the prevailing circumstances and conditions so as to make a full appraisal of the situation and of the risk of collision.

There have been cases where violations of this Rule have resulted in serious accidents. A 50-foot powerboat went hard aground on a charted and buoyed rock pile while the two-man crew was below. Apparently they left the helm unattended, depending solely on the performance of the autopilot—The Editors.

RULE 6. SAFE SPEED

Every vessel shall at all times proceed at a safe speed so that she can take proper and effective action to avoid collision and be stopped within a distance appropriate to the prevailing circumstances and conditions.

In determining a safe speed the following factors shall be among those taken into account:

(a)　By all vessels:

　　(i)　The state of visibility;

　　(ii)　The traffic density including concentrations of fishing vessels or any other vessels;

　　(iii)　The manageability of the vessel with special reference to stopping distance and turning ability in the prevailing conditions;

　　(iv)　At night, the presence of background light such as from shore lights or from back scatter from her own lights;

　　(v)　The state of wind, sea and current, and the proximity of navigational hazards;

(vi) The draft in relation to the available depth of water.

(b) Additionally, by vessels with operational radar:

(i) The characteristics, efficiency and limitations of the radar equipment;

(ii) Any constraints imposed by the radar range scale in use;

(iii) The effect on radar detection of the sea state, weather and other sources of interference;

(iv) The possibility that small vessels, ice and other floating objects may not be detected by radar at an adequate range;

(v) The number, location and movement of vessels detected by radar;

(vi) The more exact assessment of the visibility that may be possible when radar is used to determine the range of vessels or other objects in the vicinity.

This is a beauty for it requires all captains to maintain a safe speed to avoid collision and to stop before one occurs. Here again the Rules call for the use of radar to determine operating conditions. The (a) part of this Rule is often violated when operating in fog. Boats, even ships, have been known to continue at high speeds when conditions deteriorate. And relying solely on radar without cutting speed can be dangerous, as evidenced by several ship collisions in the past—The Editors.

RULE 7. RISK OF COLLISION

(a) Every vessel shall use all available means appropriate to the prevailing circumstances and conditions to determine if risk of collision exists. If there is any doubt such risk shall be deemed to exist.

(b)   Proper use shall be made of radar equipment if fitted and operational, including long-range scanning to obtain early warning of risk of collision and radar plotting or equivalent systematic observation of detected objects.

Here's another reference to RADAR. Some people may say that if the radar is turned off it is not "operational." Not so. It's assumed that if there's a radar on board and it is working properly (operational) it will be used as one of the tools for determining the risk of collision. Practice using your radar on clear days so you'll be able to use it correctly when conditions close in—The Editors.

(c)   Assumptions shall not be made on the basis of scanty information, especially scanty radar information.

(d)   In determining if risk of collision exists the following considerations shall be among those taken into account:

   (i)   Such risk shall be deemed to exist if the compass bearing of an approaching vessel does not appreciably change;

Even though this boat appears to have the right-of-way, it would be prudent not to challenge the oncoming freighter.

(ii) Such risk may sometimes exist even when an appreciable bearing change is evident, particularly when approaching a very large vessel or a tow or when approaching a vessel at close range.

RULE 8. ACTION TO AVOID COLLISION

(a) Any action taken to avoid collision shall *be taken in accordance with the Rules of this Part and shall* **INTL** (effective 11/29/02), if the circumstances of the case admit, be positive, made in ample time and with due regard to the observance of good seamanship.

(b) Any alteration of course and/or speed to avoid collision shall, if the circumstances of the case admit, be large enough to be readily apparent to another vessel observing visually or by radar; a succession of small alterations of course and/or speed should be avoided.

Most recreational skippers seem to resist making changes in course and speed, especially if running on autopilot or tracking down a GPS waypoint route. If you're required to give way (Rules 16 & 17) be sure you do so early enough and significantly enough to eliminate confusion or worry on the part of the other helmsman. Waiting until the last minute in an attempt to judge whether or not you can safely pass ahead of a privileged vessel is risky business, especially if you're playing chicken with a big ship. Make it a practice to go astern and make your intention known with an early turn and reduction in speed. Small alterations in course and speed are cautioned against in Rule 8b—The Editors.

(c) If there is sufficient sea room, alteration of course alone may be the most effective action to avoid a close-quarters situation provided that it is made in good time, is substantial and does not result in another close-quarters situation.

(d) Action taken to avoid collision with another vessel shall be such as to result in passing at a safe distance. The effective ness of the action shall be carefully checked until the other vessel is finally past and clear.

(e) If necessary to avoid collision or allow more time to assess the situation, a vessel may slacken her speed or take all way off by stopping or reversing her means of propulsion.

(f) (i) A vessel which, by any of these rules, is required not to impede the passage or safe passage of another vessel shall, when required by the circumstances of the case, take early action to allow sufficient sea room for the safe passage of the other vessel.

(ii) A vessel required not to impede the passage or safe passage of another vessel is not relieved of this obligation if approaching the other vessel so as to involve risk of collision and shall, when taking action, have full regard to the action, which may be required by the rules of this part.

Paragraphs f(i) and (ii) talk to the helmsman aboard the boat that must stay out of the way of the other vessel; f(iii) talks to the helmsman who has the right-of-way. He's aboard the stand-on vessel, and its actions are governed by Rule 12—The Editors.

(iii) A vessel, the passage of which is not to be impeded remains fully obliged to comply with the rules of this part when the two vessels are approaching one another so as to involve risk of collision. **(See Rule 12.)**

RULE 9. NARROW CHANNELS

(a) *(i)* **INLD** A vessel proceeding along the course of a narrow channel or fairway shall keep as near to the outer limit of the channel or fairway which lies on her starboard side as is safe and practicable.

This sentence reads exactly the same in the International Rules. The only difference is the (i) in the Inland Rules is used to announce the addition of another paragraph that does not appear in the International Rules—The Editors.

(ii) Notwithstanding paragraph (a)(i) and Rule 14(a), a power-driven vessel operating in narrow channels or fairways on the Great Lakes, Western Rivers, or waters specified by the Secretary, and proceeding downbound with a following current shall have the right-of-way over an upbound vessel, shall propose the manner and place of passage, and shall initiate the maneuvering signals prescribed by Rule 34(a)(i), as appropriate. The vessel proceeding upbound against the current shall hold as necessary to permit safe passing. **INLD**

This is about the only actual reference in the Inland Rules to right-of-way. In all other cases the phrases "stand-on," "give-way," "shall not impede," and "shall keep out of the way of" are used. It's this Rule 9(a)(ii) that some skippers point to during strong tidal flows at bridges when boats line up on both the up-tide and down-tide sides. Though the Rule does not talk about tidal waters, it's a fact that those running with the tide sometimes have more difficulty maneuvering than those stemming the current. When a bridge opens, some skippers support the concept that vessels running with the tide should have the right of way and come through first. Others don't—The Editors.

(b) A vessel of less than 20 meters **(65.6 ft.)** in length or a sail ing vessel shall not impede the passage of a vessel which can safely navigate only within a narrow channel or fair way.

For recreational boaters this Rule presents some challenges, especially when navigating in narrow channels along with ships and tugs moving multiple barges. For sailors, claiming "privilege" over a ship is not only illegal but often stupid. Though they appear to be traveling at a slow rate of speed, some ships are, in fact, moving faster than you might think. For sailors a sudden drop in wind, or for power boaters, an unexpected breakdown in the path of a large vessel, can ruin your day. Large commercial vessels cannot stop on a dime. Sometimes it requires miles. Remember, too, rugged cables always connect tugs to towed barges. The best advice is to stay clear of all vessels substantially larger than you. Circle around behind. Slow down and let them pass. Tack or turn to head away from them. The Rules are written to lessen the risk of collision, not to guarantee privilege—The Editors.

(c)   A vessel engaged in fishing shall not impede the passage of any other vessel navigating within a narrow channel or fairway. **[See Rule 9(g)]**

(d)   A vessel shall not cross a narrow passage or fairway if such crossing impedes the passage of a vessel which can safely navigate only within such channel or fairway. The latter vessel may use the sound signal prescribed in Rule 34(d) **(the danger signal, five short and rapid blasts)** if in doubt as to the intention of the crossing vessel.

(e)

INTERNATIONAL	INLAND
(i) In a narrow channel or fairway when overtaking can take place only if the vessel to be overtaken has to take action to permit safe passing, the vessel intending to overtake shall indicate her intention by sounding the appropriate signal prescribed in Rule 34(c)(i). The vessel to be overtaken shall, if in agreement, sound the appropri-	(i) In a narrow channel or fairway when overtaking, the power-driven vessel intending to overtake another power-driven vessel shall indicate her intention by sounding the appropriate signal prescribed in Rule 34(c) and take steps to permit safe passing. The power-driven vessel being overtaken, if in agreement, shall sound the same signal

INTERNATIONAL	INLAND
ate signal prescribed in Rule 34(c)(ii) and take steps to permit safe passing. If in doubt she may sound the signals prescribed in Rule 34(d).	and may, if specifically agreed to take steps to permit safe passing. If in doubt, she shall sound the danger signal prescribed in Rule 34(d).

There are two significant differences between International and Inland Rules when looking at 9(e)(i). The first involves the specific reference of "power-driven vessel" in Inland and the absence of such defining language in International. In both Rules, paragraph 9(b) makes it absolutely clear that power-driven vessels under 65.6 ft. (20 meters) and sailing vessels must keep clear of a vessel that can safely navigate only in a narrow channel or fairway. The second difference deals with overtaking in a narrow channel. In 9(e)(i) of International, certain signals are called for "only if the vessel to be overtaken has to take action to permit safe passing...." In 9 (e)(i) of the Inland Rules, signals are required when simply "intending to overtake...." Though the meaning is the same, the actual signals differ. International Rules call for the overtaking vessel to sound the following signals: two prolonged and one short blast to mean, "I intend to overtake you on your starboard side"; two prolonged and two short blasts to mean, "I intend to overtake you on your port side." If the vessel being overtaken agrees it should sound "one prolonged, one short, one prolonged and one short" blast. This is the Morse code letter "C," meaning "yes."

The Inland Rules call for different and simpler signals: one short blast to mean, "I intend to overtake you on your starboard side;" two short blasts to mean, "I intend to overtake you on your port side." If the overtaken vessel agrees, it sounds the same signal.

In both International and Inland Rules the overtaken vessel is required to signal at least five short and rapid blasts should it not agree or be in doubt. This is the danger signal called for in Rule 34(d).

You'll notice that "I intend" are the operating words in both sets of Rules. You'll see later on that when maneuvering "I intend" is only used in Inland Rules, while the declaratory "I am" maneuvering is used in International Rules. In both cases the actual signals are the same. [See Rule 34(a)].

In actual practice, recreational boaters who overtake one another in congested waters on sunny weekends seldom observe these Rules. In case of an accident, however, failure to observe the Rules will not work in anyone's favor.

In rivers and waterways, when recreational boats meet commercial ships and tugs communications is usually done not by signals but by VHF radio using Channel 16/13 [Rule 34(h)]. A tug captain really appreciates this effort, especially if he's pushing ahead a raft of barges. He may have to swing wide on a turn obstructing your way. He may worry about the wake from a large pleasure boat stressing his cables. Passing or overtaking anyone at a slow bell is always appreciated. And selecting a side to pass is usually negotiated. "How about two whistles, Cap?" "No. Better come up on one." [See Rule 34(c)] "One whistle it is."

Rule 34 will be covered in more detail later on, but remember that according to the Rules the same whistle signal can signify different maneuvers when passing, crossing or overtaking. When passing or crossing, one whistle in International Rules means, "I am altering my course to starboard." When overtaking it means, "I intend to overtake you on your starboard side." In Inland Rules one whistle can mean two things. When crossing or passing it can mean: "I intend to leave you on my port side"; when overtaking: "I intend to overtake you on your starboard side." Two and three short blasts are further explained in Rule 34(a) and (c)—The Editors.

(ii) This rule does not relieve the overtaking vessel of her obligation under Rule 13.

(f) A vessel nearing a bend or an area of a narrow channel or fairway where other vessels may be obscured by an intervening obstruction shall navigate with particular alertness and caution and shall sound the appropriate signal prescribed in Rule 34(e).

A vessel heading downstream and nearing a bend announces its presence by sounding one prolonged blast. An upstream vessel responds in kind. Today VHF radios are used to communicate similar information. See Rule 34 (h).

(g) Any vessel shall, if the circumstances of the case admit, avoid anchoring in a narrow channel.

In some parts of the country recreational fishermen in small skiffs, rowboats or center consoles anchor right in the middle of narrow channels forcing larger boats to come dangerously close to the shallows. This is especially true in Long Island's Great South Bay and along the Intracoastal Waterway. Even though the fishing is better in these spots, Rule 9(c) and (g) apply—The Editors.

RULE 10. TRAFFIC SEPARATION SCHEMES

(a)   This Rule applies to traffic separation schemes *adopted by the Organization* **INTL** and does not relieve any vessel of her obligation under any other rule.

(b)   A vessel using a traffic separation scheme shall:

    (i)   Proceed in the appropriate traffic lane in the general direction of traffic flow for that lane.

The shaded lane separates the inbound from the outbound traffic lanes. This chart shows three such arrangements along the approaches to New York Harbor.

    (ii)   So far as is practicable keep clear of a traffic separation line or separation zone.

    (iii) Normally join or leave a traffic lane at the termination of the lane, but when joining or leaving from either side shall do so at as small an angle to the general direction of traffic flow as practicable.

(c)   A vessel, shall so far as practicable, avoid crossing traffic lanes but if obliged to do so shall cross on a heading as nearly as practicable at right angles to the general direction of traffic flow.

(d)   (i)   A vessel shall not use an inshore traffic zone when she can safely use the appropriate traffic lane within the adjacent traffic separation scheme. However, vessels of less than 20 meters **(65.6 ft.)** in length, sailing vessels and vessels engaged in fishing may use the inshore traffic zone.

        (ii) Notwithstanding subparagraph (d)(i), a vessel may use an inshore traffic zone when en route to or from a port, offshore installation or structure, pilot station or any other place situated within the inshore traffic zone, or to avoid immediate danger.

(e)   A vessel, other than a crossing vessel or a vessel joining or leaving a lane shall not normally enter a separation zone or cross a separation line except:

        (i)   in cases of emergency to avoid immediate danger;

        (ii) to engage in fishing within a separation zone.

(f)   A vessel navigating in areas near the terminations of traffic separation schemes shall do so with particular caution.

(g)   A vessel shall so far as practicable avoid anchoring in a traffic separation scheme or in areas near its terminations.

(h)   A vessel not using a traffic separating scheme shall avoid it by as wide a margin as is practicable.

(i)   A vessel engaged in fishing shall not impede the passage of any vessel following a traffic lane.

(j)   A vessel of less than 20 meters **(65.6 ft.)** in length or a sailing vessel shall not impede the safe passage of a power-driven vessel following a traffic lane.

(k)   A vessel restricted in her ability to maneuver when engaged in an operation for the maintenance of safety of navigation in a traffic separation scheme is exempted from complying with this Rule to the extent necessary to carry out the operation.

(l)   A vessel restricted in her ability to maneuver when engaged in an operation for the laying, servicing or pick ing up of a submarine cable, within a traffic separation scheme, is exempted from complying with this Rule to the extent necessary to carry out the operation.

PART B, STEERING AND SAILING RULES
SECTION II/SUBPART II
CONDUCT OF VESSELS IN SIGHT OF ONE ANOTHER
Rules 11-18

RULE 11/12. APPLCATION / SAILING VESSELS

Rule 11

Rules in this section apply to vessels in sight of one another.

Rule 12

(a)   When two sailing vessels are approaching one another, so as to involve risk of collision, one of them shall keep out of the way of the other as follows:

(i)   when each has the wind on a different side, the vessel which has the wind on the port side shall keep out of the way of the other;

(ii)   when both have the wind on the same side, the vessel which is to windward shall keep out of the way of the vessel which is to leeward;

(iii) if a vessel with the wind on the port side sees a vessel to windward and cannot determine with certainty whether the other vessel has the wind on the port or on the starboard side, she shall keep out of the way of the other.

(b)   For the purposes of this Rule the windward side shall be deemed to be the side opposite that on which the main sail is carried or, in the case of a square-rigged vessel, the side opposite to that on which the largest fore-and-aft sail is carried.

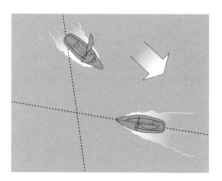

Wind over the same side, the windward boat stays clear. Wind over different sides, the boat with the wind over the port side stays clear.

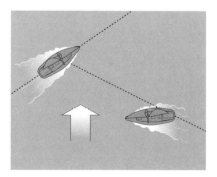

(a)   Notwithstanding anything contained in the Rules [of Part B, Sections I and II / 4 through 18], any vessel overtaking any other shall keep out of the way of the vessel being overtaken.

(b)   A vessel shall be deemed to be overtaking when coming up with another vessel from a direction more than 22.5 degrees abaft her beam; that is, in such a position with reference to the vessel she is overtaking, that at night she would be able to see only the sternlight of that vessel but neither of her sidelights.

(c)   When a vessel is in any doubt as to whether she is over taking another, she shall assume that this is the case and act accordingly.

(d)   Any subsequent alteration of the bearing between the two vessels shall not make the overtaking vessel a crossing vessel within the meaning of these Rules or relieve her of the duty of keeping clear of the overtaken vessel until she is finally past and clear.

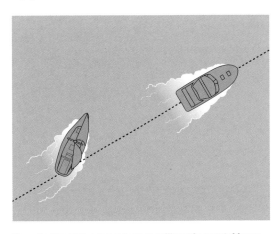

Even in the rare case where a sailboat is overtaking a powerboat, the Rules establishing the "overtaking vessel" are clear be it either power or sail.

Rule 14

(a)   *Unless otherwise agreed* **INLD** When two power-driven vessels are meeting on reciprocal or nearly reciprocal courses so as to involve risk of collision each shall alter her course to starboard so that each shall pass on the portside of the other.

(b)   Such a situation shall be deemed to exist when a vessel sees the other ahead or nearly ahead and by night she could see the masthead lights of the other in a line or nearly in a line *and/* **INTL** or both sidelights and by day she observes the corresponding aspect of the other vessel.

(c)   When a vessel is in any doubt as to whether such a situation exists she shall assume that it does exist and act accordingly.

(d)   *Notwithstanding paragraph (a) of this Rule, a power-driven vessel operating on the Great Lakes, Western Rivers, or waters specified by the Secretary, and proceeding downbound with a following current shall have the right-of-way over an upbound vessel, shall propose the manner of passage, and shall initiate the maneuvering signals prescribed by Rule 34(a)(i), as appropriate.* **INLD See COMMENTS under Rule 9 (a)(ii)]**

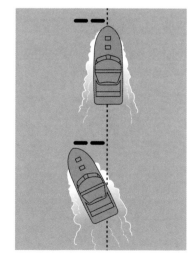

Portside passing is the norm. This Rule also supports Rule 9(a)(i) that calls for a vessel to favor the limit of a narrow channel or fairway that's on her starboard side, and Rule 17(c), which calls for alterations to starboard with a vessel to port.

Rule 15

When two power-driven vessels are crossing so as to involve risk of collision, the vessel which has the other on her own starboard side shall keep out of the way and shall, if the circumstances of the case admit, avoid crossing ahead of the other vessel.

So clear yet so often abused by recreational boaters, this is the situation in which boaters most often find themselves. Note the reference here to "power-driven vessels." Under Rule 18(a)(iv), sailboats can claim the right-of-way and cause powerboats to give way. Actions of the give-way boat, be it faced with either a sail or another powerboat in the stand-on (Rule 17) or right-of-way position, are also affected by other Rules. Remember, Rule 8(f)(i) requires positive and early action be taken [Rule 8(a) & Rule 16], including slowing, stopping, or reversing [Rule 8(e)]. Remember, too, that course and speed changes should be "substantial" [Rule 8(c)] and obvious even on radar [Rule 8(b)]. Small alterations of course and speed should be avoided [Rule 8(b)]. And finally, Rule 15 calls for the give way boat to go astern of the privileged one and "avoid crossing ahead...."—The Editors.

(b)   *Notwithstanding paragraph (a), on the Great Lakes, Western Rivers, or water specified by the Secretary, a power-driven vessel crossing a river shall keep out of the way of a power-driven vessel ascending or descending the river.* **INLD**

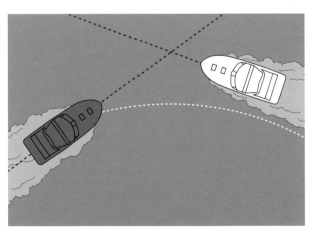

The powerboat with another vessel off its starboard side must give-way in a crossing situation.

RULE 16/17. ACTION BY GIVE-WAY/ STAND- ON VESSEL

For all mariners these two Rules are probably the most important of all. They define the actions and the burdens of vessels, including recreational boats, as they encounter each other in all conditions of visibility—The Editors.

Rule 16 ACTION BY THE GIVE-WAY VESSEL

Every vessel which is directed to keep out of the way of another vessel shall, so far as possible, take early and substantial action to keep well clear.

Originally known as the burdened vessel clause, this Rule lays out the actions to be taken by a boat labeled the "give-way vessel." The operative phrase is to "keep out of the way..." as stated in a number of the Steering and Sailing Rules. Under this Rule 16 any boat tagged as the give-way vessel must take early and substantial action so that its maneuvering is obvious to the other vessel even when viewed on radar. Other Rules including Rule 8(a), (b), (c), (f)(i) and Rule 9(e) underscore this "early and substantial" phrase—The Editors.

Rule 17 ACTION BY THE STAND-ON VESSEL

(a) (i) Where one of two vessels is to keep out of the way, the other shall keep her course and speed.

This obtuse language defines the vessel with the right-of-way—a term rarely used in the Rules. In the past it has also been labeled the "privileged vessel" and now it's the "Stand-on Vessel Rule." International maritime treaties dictate many of these changes.

But it's the phrase "shall keep her course and speed" that causes the most problems among recreational boaters. There is little trouble in open waters, but in rivers, harbors and waterways (such as sections of the Intracoastal and Inside Passage) a skipper's dedication to maintaining course and speed, especially speed, has resulted in confrontations. It usually happens during an overtaking situation when a powerboat tries to get by a sailboat in a narrow channel. It is true that some power captains blast by without regard to the signaling or safe speed Rules, or to the damaging effects of their wakes. But for the most part the overtaking can be done without incident, especially if the sailboat abandons the course and speed mandate and slows in favor of a safer and more comfortable passage. Reread Rule 2. Maintaining course and speed often forces a powerboat to pass at an eight-, nine-, or 10-knot speed where wakes are at their worst. Slowing to five knots or less eliminates that problem. As soon as the powerboat passes, the sailboat should turn toward the wake and cross into the slipstream. This move shortens the passing time, maintains a stable sailboat, and allows the powerboat to speed up. Its developing wake will not affect the sailboat—The Editors.

(ii) The latter vessel may however take action to avoid collision by her maneuver alone, as soon as it becomes apparent to her that the vessel required to keep out of the way is not taking appropriate action in compliance with these Rules.

(b) When, from any cause, the vessel required to keep her course and speed finds herself so close that collision cannot be avoided by the action of the give-way vessel alone, she shall take such action as will best aid to avoid collision.

(c) A power-driven vessel which takes action in a crossing situation in accordance with subparagraph (a)(ii) of this Rule to avoid collision with another power-driven vessel shall, if the circumstances of the case admit, not alter course to port for a vessel on her own port side.

(d) This Rule does not relieve the give-way vessel of her obligation to keep out of the way.

RULE 18. RESPONSIBILITIES BETWEEN VESSELS //

Here's the pecking order. This list establishes the relationship of certain vessels to one another. It does this by establishing when each of the three classifications of vessel—power-driven, sailing and fishing (commercial), —should become the give-way vessel —The Editors.

Except where Rules 9, 10, and 13 otherwise require:

(a)   A power-driven vessel underway shall keep out of the way of:

   (i)   a vessel not under command; **(known as a NUC, unofficially)**

   (ii) a vessel restricted in her ability to maneuver; **(called a RAM, unofficially)**

   (iii) a vessel engaged in fishing;

   (iv) a sailing vessel.

(b)   A sailing vessel underway shall keep out of the way of:

   (i)   a vessel not under command;

   (ii) a vessel restricted in her ability to maneuver;

   (iii) a vessel engaged in fishing.

(c)   A vessel engaged in fishing when underway shall, so far as possible, keep out of the way of:

   (i)   a vessel not under command;

   (ii) a vessel restricted in her ability to maneuver.

(d/)   (i)   *Any vessel other than a vessel not under command or a vessel restricted in her ability to maneuver shall, if the circumstances of the case admit, avoid impeding the safe passage of a vessel constrained by her draft* **(known unofficially as a COD),** *exhibiting the signals in Rule 28.* **INTL**

        (ii) *A vessel constrained by her draft shall navigate with particular caution having full regard to her special condition.* **INTL** (e/d) A seaplane on the water shall, in general, keep well clear of all vessels and avoid impeding their navigation. In circumstances, however, where risk of collision exists, she shall comply with the Rules of this Part.

(f) (i) *A WIG craft shall, when taking off, landing and in flight near the surface, keep well clear of all other vessels and avoid impeding their navigation;* **INTL** (effective 11/29/03)

(ii) *A WIG craft operating on the water surface shall comply with the Rules of this Part as a power-driven vessel.* **INTL** (effective 11/29/03)

PART B, STEERING AND SAILING RULES
Section III/Subpart III
CONDUCT OF VESSELS IN RESTRICTED VISIBILITY

RULE 19. CONDUCT OF VESSELS IN RESTRICTED VISIBILITY

(a) This Rule applies to vessels not in sight of one another when navigating in or near an area of restricted visibility.

Remember that Rule 3(k) defines "restricted visibility" as "...any condition in which visibility is restricted by fog, mist, falling snow, heavy rainstorms, sandstorms, any other similar causes" —The Editors.

(b) Every vessel shall proceed at a safe speed adapted to the prevailing circumstances and conditions of restricted visibility. A power-driven vessel shall have her engines ready for immediate maneuver.

(c) Every vessel shall have due regard to the prevailing circumstances and conditions of restricted visibility when complying with *Rules 4 through 10* **INLD** *the Rules of Section I of this Part* **INTL**.

As most "restricted visibility" for recreational boats involves fog, Rule 5 becomes very important. It states that "a proper look-out by sight and hearing" is required to avoid collisions. The sounding of fog signals is dealt with in Rule 35—The Editors.

(d)   A vessel which detects by radar alone the presence of another vessel shall determine if a close-quarters situation is developing *and/* **INTL** or risk of collision exists. If so, she shall take avoiding action in ample time, provided that when such action consists of an alteration in course, so far as possible the following shall be avoided:

      (i)   an alteration of course to port for a vessel forward of the beam, other than for a vessel being overtaken;

      (ii)   an alteration of course toward a vessel abeam or abaft the beam.

Remember Rule 7(b), which calls for the use of radar to determine if the risk of collision exists. If you have it, use it—The Editors.

(e)   Except where it has been determined that a risk of collision does not exist, every vessel which hears apparently forward of her beam the fog signal of another vessel, or which cannot avoid a close-quarters situation with another vessel forward of her beam, shall reduce her speed to be the minimum at which she can be kept on her course. She shall if necessary take all her way off and, in any event, navigate with extreme caution until danger of collision is over.

PART C, LIGHTS AND SHAPES

Rules 20-31

These Rules specify the running lights that will be shown from "sunset to sunrise" by vessels of different designs and sizes. It's important for a skipper of a recreational boat to recognize them, especially when operating at night or during times of restricted visibility in the daytime when running lights are also required. Presumably the manufacturers fit recreational boats with the proper running lights, although it doesn't hurt to check.

Some vessels, such as sailboats operating under sail and power, are called upon to display day shapes. The value of this Part C is in the ability of a helmsman to understand the type of vessel he is about to encounter. Is it a dinghy under oars with a handheld light or is it a freighter coming at him? Though it's necessary to recognize the running lights of other recreational boats, both power and sail, it's even more important to decipher the running lights of tugs with barges, particularly when those barges are being towed. Many an accident or close encounter has occurred because the skipper of a recreational boat did not realize that a tug and barges in tow are connected by a cable that could be from a quarter- to a half-mile long.

Study these Rules and remember those light configurations that will most likely appear in your cruising waters. These could include other powerboats and sailboats, small craft such as inflatables, and tugs and barges. It's not likely you'll see a minesweeper or a dracone. But you could come across a log raft in the Northwest or a pilot boat off New York Harbor. This is why you should have a copy of these Rules handy. If you are in a boat more than 39.4 ft. (12 meters) operating in Inland waters, a copy of the Rules is required aboard (Annex V, Section 88.05)—The Editors.

RULE 20. APPLICATION

(a)   Rules in this Part shall be complied with in all weathers.

(b)   The Rules concerning lights shall be complied with from sunset to sunrise, and during such times no other lights shall be exhibited, except such lights which cannot be mistaken for the lights specified in these Rules or do not impair their visibility or distinctive character, or interfere with the keeping of a proper look-out.

(c)   The lights prescribed by these Rules shall, if carried, also be exhibited from sunrise to sunset in restricted visibility and may be exhibited in all other circumstances when it is deemed necessary.

(d)   The Rules concerning shapes shall be complied with by day.

The black "at anchor" ball is the most common day shape you'll see [Rule 30(a)(i)]. You may even see a basket used to designate a commercial fishing boat though that symbol has officially been discarded by the Rules. For those cruising in waters where dredges are operating it may be necessary to refer to the day shapes [Rule 27(d)] to determine safe water. Remember: "Diamonds are a girl's best friend." Diamond-shaped day markers indicate the passing side of a dredge—The Editors.

(e)   The lights and shapes specified in these Rules shall comply with the provisions of Annex I *of these Rules* **INLD** *to these Regulations* **INTL**.

RULE 21. DEFINITIONS

(a)   "Masthead light" means a white light placed over the fore and aft centerline of the vessel showing an unbroken light over an arc of the horizon of 225 degrees and so fixed as to show the light from right ahead to 22.5 degrees abaft the beam on either side of the vessel, *except that on a vessel of less than 12 meters* **(39.4 ft.)** *in length the masthead light shall be placed as nearly as practicable to the fore and aft center line of the vessel.* **INLD**

(b)   "Sidelights" means a green light on the starboard side and a red light on the port side each showing an unbroken light over an arc of the horizon of 112.5 degrees and so fixed as to show the light from right ahead to 22.5 degrees abaft the beam on its respective side. On a vessel of less than 20 meters **(65.6 ft.)** in length the sidelights may be combined in one lantern carried on the fore and aft centerline of the

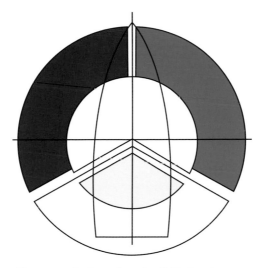

The arcs and colors of running lights found on both commercial and recreational vessels. Recreational boats do not use the yellow light reserved for tugs involved in towing operations.

vessel, *except that on a vessel of less than 12 meters* **(39.4 ft.)** *in length the sidelights when combined in one lantern shall be placed as nearly as practicable to the fore and aft centerline of the vessel.* **INLD**

(c)   "Sternlight" means a white light placed as nearly as practicable at the stern showing an unbroken light over an arc of the horizon of 135 degrees and so fixed as to show the light 67.5 degrees from right aft on each side of the vessel.

(d)   "Towing light" means a yellow light having the same characteristics as the "sternlight" defined in paragraph (c) of this Rule.

(e)   "All-round light" means a light showing an unbroken light over an arc of the horizon of 360 degrees.

(f)   "Flashing light" means a light flashing at regular intervals at a frequency of 120 flashes or more per minute.

(g)   *"Special flashing light" means a yellow light flashing at regular intervals at a frequency of 50 to 70 flashes per minute, placed as far forward and as nearly as practicable on the fore and aft center line of the tow and showing an unbroken light over an arc of the horizon of not less than 180 degrees nor more than 225 degrees and so fixed as to show the light from right ahead to abeam and no more than 22.5 degrees abaft the beam on either side of the vessel.* **INLD**

RULE 22. VISIBILITY OF LIGHTS

The lights prescribed in these Rules shall have an intensity as specified in *Section 8* **INTL** of Annex I to these *Rules* **INLD** *Regulations* **INTL** so as to be visible at the following minimum ranges:

(a)   In vessels of 50 meters **(164 ft.)** or more in length:

- a masthead light, 6 miles;
- a sidelight, 3 miles;
- a sternlight, 3 miles;
- a towing light, 3 miles;
- a white, red, green or yellow all-round light, 3 miles.
- *a special flashing* **(yellow)** *light, 2 miles.* **INLD**

(b)   In vessels of 12 meters **(39.4 ft.)** or more in length but less than 50 meters **(164 ft.)** in length;

- a masthead light, 5 miles; except that where the length of the vessel is less than 20 meters **(65.6 ft.)**, 3 miles;
- a sidelight, 2 miles;
- a sternlight, 2 miles;
- a towing light, 2 miles;
- a white, red, green or yellow all-round light, 2 miles.
- *a special flashing* **(yellow)** *light, 2 miles.* **INLD**

(c)   In vessels of less than 12 meters **(39.4 ft.)** in length:

- a masthead light, 2 miles;
- a sidelight, 1 mile;

- a towing light, 2 miles;
- a white, red, green or yellow all-round light, 2 miles.
- *a special flashing* **(yellow)** *light, 2 miles.* **INLD**

(d)   In an inconspicuous, partly submerged vessel or object being towed:

- a white all-round light, 3 miles.

RULE 23. POWER-DRIVEN VESSELS UNDERWAY

(a)   A power-driven vessel underway shall exhibit:

(i)   a masthead light forward;

(ii)   a second masthead light abaft of and higher than the forward one; except that a vessel of less than 50 meters **(164 ft.)** in length shall not be obliged to exhibit such a light but may do so;

Though not obliged to use such an arrangement there is little reference to what might be acceptable. Paragraph (c) in this Rule notes that an all-around white light may be used on power-driven vessels 39.4 ft. (12 meters) or less in length. It's finally in Inland Rule 38 that a clarification for larger vessels appears. Under (d)(vi) an exemption to this Inland Rule 23a (i) and (iv) allows power-driven vessels from 39.4 ft. (12 meters) to 65.6 ft. (20 meters) to show an all-around white light. This exemption is for vessels built in 1980 or earlier, but there's a hint of what might be acceptable on vessels built after 1980—The Editors.

(iii) sidelights; and

(iv)   a sternlight.

(b)   An air-cushion vessel when operating in nondisplacement mode shall, in addition to the lights prescribed in paragraph (a) of this Rule, exhibit an all-round flashing yellow light, *where it can best be seen.* **INLD** *(c/)   A WIG craft only when taking off, landing and in flight near the surface shall, in addition to the lights prescribed in paragraph (a) of this Rule, exhibit a high intensity all-round flashing red light.* **INTL**

(d(i)/c) A power-driven vessel of less than 12 meters **(39.4 ft.)** in length may, in lieu of the lights prescribed in paragraph (a) of this Rule, exhibit an all-round white light and sidelights.

*(ii)   a power-driven vessel of less than 7 meters **(23 ft.)** in length whose maximum speed does not exceed 7 knots may in lieu of the lights prescribed in paragraph (a) of this Rule exhibit an all-round white light and shall, if practicable, also exhibit sidelights;* **INTL**

Under both International and Inland Rules a powerboat under **39.4 ft. (12 meters)** can have all-around white lights and side-lights. Under International Rules a powerboat under 23 ft. whose speed is no greater than 7 knots need exhibit only an all-around white light. Sidelights may be shown if practicable. This exemption does not apply to a powerboat operated under the Inland Rules where a white light and sidelights are required on all power-driven vessels. Small, open sailboats under 23 ft. and all boats propelled by oars need not show running lights as long as they carry flashlights and display the lights in enough time to prevent collision. Rule 25(d)—The Editors.

---

*(iii)   the masthead light or all-round white light on a power-driven vessel of less than 12 meters **(39.4 ft.)** in length may be displaced from the fore and aft centerline of the vessel if centerline fitting is not practicable, provided the sidelights are combined in one lantern which shall be carried on the fore and aft centerline of the vessel or located as nearly as practicable in the same fore and aft line as the masthead light or the all-round white light.* **INTL**

---

1 Submarines may display, as a distinctive means of identification, an intermittent flashing amber (yellow) beacon with a sequence of operation of one flash per second for three (3) seconds followed by a three (3) second off-period. Other special rules made by the Secretary of the Navy with respect to additional station and signal lights are found in Part 706 of Title 32, Code of Federal Regulations (32 CFR 706).

This International Rule allows the off-center location of a white light provided the port and starboard sidelights are combined into one fixture. Inland Rules allow off-center whites and combined sidelights but don't require the sidelights be in one fixture —The Editors.

Rule 23a
Power-driven vessel underway.

Rule 23
Power-driven vessel underway, less than 50 meters (164 ft.) in length.

Rule 23b
Air-cushion vessel underway operating in the nondisplacement mode - vessel less than 50 meters (164 ft.) in length.

Rule 23b
Air-cushion vessel underway operating in the displacement mode - vessel less than 50 meters (164 ft.) in length.

Rule 23d/c
Power-driven vessel underway less than 12 meters (39.4 ft.) in length.

Rule 23d
Power-driven vessel underway less than 7 meters (23 ft.) in length whose maximum speed does not exceed 7 knots. International Only

(d)   A power-driven vessel when operating on the Great Lakes may
       carry an all-round white light in lieu of the second masthead light
       and sternlight prescribed in paragraph (a) of this Rule. The light
    shall be carried in the position of the second masthead light and
              be visible at the same minimum range. **INLD**

Rule 23d
**In addition to the normal running lights of a power-driven vessel, a submarine may
display a yellow flashing beacon.**

RULE 24. TOWING AND PUSHING

By far, this is one of the most important Rules because it deals
with tugs, be they pushing, pulling, or towing barges alongside.
When towing, tugs and barges are separated from one another,
connected only by a thick steel cable that usually runs submerged
between them. Too many recreational boat skippers have unknow-
ingly steamed into the cable, not realizing or fully understanding
what danger lies ahead. This danger is especially real at night. So,
more attention should be given to understanding how tugs and
barges are lit at night. The main difference between International
and Inland Rules comes in the use of yellow tow lights and special
flashing (yellow) lights. On tugs towing barges astern, a single yellow
light above a single white sternlight is required under both Rules.
On tugs pushing or towing alongside, the lighting requirements
change. Under International Rules only a white sternlight is needed.
Under Inland Rules, two yellow tow lights and no white sternlight
are required. Special flashing (yellow) lights are also required on
the bows of barges pushed or carried alongside in Inland waters.
Under both Rules, normal red and green sidelights are needed on
all barges being towed astern, pushed, or alongside. White sternlights are used on barges on all but push-ahead rigs—The Editors.

(a)   A power-driven vessel when towing *astern* **INLD** shall
       exhibit:

(i) instead of the light prescribed in Rule 23(a)(i) or 23(a)(ii), two masthead lights in a vertical line. When the length of the tow, measuring from the stern of the towing vessel to the after end of the tow exceeds 200 meters **(656.2 ft.)**, three such lights in a vertical line;

(ii) sidelights;

(iii) a sternlight;

(iv) a towing light in a vertical line above the stern light; and

(v) when the length of the tow exceeds 200 meters **(656.2 ft.)**, a diamond shape where it can best be seen.

Tugs, when running offshore, will often increase the distance between themselves and their tows to lessen the strain on the cables in developing seas. You can see the confusion the skipper of a recreational boat might have if he does not recognize that the two are linked together by a submerged steel cable—The Editors.

(b) When a pushing vessel and a vessel being pushed ahead are rigidly connected in a composite unit they shall be regarded as a power-driven vessel and exhibit the lights prescribed in Rule 23.

(c) A power-driven vessel when pushing ahead or towing alongside, except *in the case of a composite unit* **INTL** *as required by paragraphs (b) and (i) of this Rule* **INLD**, shall exhibit:

(i) instead of the light prescribed in Rule 23(a)(i) or 23(a)(ii), two masthead lights in a vertical line;

(ii) sidelights; and

(iii) *a sternlight* **INTL** *two towing lights in a vertical line* **INLD**.

(d)   A power-driven vessel to which paragraph (a) or (c) of this Rule apply shall also comply with rule *23(a)(i)* **INLD** and 23(a)(ii).

(e)   A vessel or object being towed, other than those mentioned in paragraph (g) of this Rule, shall exhibit:

    (i)   sidelights;

    (ii)   a sternlight;

    (iii)   when the length of the tow exceeds 200 meters **(656.2 ft.),** a diamond shape where it can best be seen.

(f)   Provided that any number of vessels **(usually barges)** being towed alongside or pushed in a group shall be lighted as one vessel, *except as provided in paragraph (iii)* **INLD**:

    (i)   a vessel **(usually a barge)** being pushed ahead, not being part of a composite unit, shall exhibit at the forward end, sidelights, *and a special flashing light* **INLD**;

    (ii)   a vessel **(usually a barge)** being towed alongside shall exhibit a sternlight and at the forward end, sidelights, *and a special flashing light* **INLD**;

(iii)   when vessels **(here, too, usually barges)** *are towed alongside on both sides of the towing vessels a sternlight shall be exhibited on the stern of the outboard vessel on each side of the towing vessel, and a single set of sidelights as far forward and as far outboard as is practicable, and a single special flashing light* **INLD**.

(g)   An inconspicuous, partly submerged vessel or object, or *combination of such vessels or objects being towed,* **INTL** shall exhibit:

INTERNATIONAL	INLAND
(i) if it is less than 25 meters (82 ft.) in breadth, one all-round white light at or near the forward end and one at or near the after end except that dracones need not exhibit a light at or near the forward end;	(i) if it is less than 25 meters (82 ft.) in breadth, one all-round white light at or near each end;
(ii) if it is 25 meters (82 ft.) or more in breadth, two or more additional all-round white lights at or near the extremities of its breadth;	(ii) if it is 25 meters (82 ft.) or more in breadth, four all-round white lights to mark its length and breadth;

(iii) if it exceeds 100 meters **(328.1 ft.)** in length, additonal all-round white lights between the lights prescribed in sub-paragraphs (i) and (ii) so that the distance between the lights shall not exceed 100 meters **(328.1 ft.).** *Provided, that any vessels or objects being towed alongside each other shall be lighted as one vessel or object* **INLD**;

      (iv)   a diamond shape at or near the aftermost extremity of the last vessel or object being towed and *if the length of the tow exceeds 200 meters* **(656.2 ft.)** *an additional diamond shape where it can best be seen and located as far forward as is practicable* **INTL**;

      (v)   the towing vessel may direct a searchlight in the direction of the tow to indicate its presence to an approaching vessel **INLD**;

(h)   Where from any sufficient cause it is impracticable for a vessel or object being towed to exhibit the lights *or shapes* **INTL** prescribed in paragraph (e) or (g) of this Rule, all possible measures shall be taken to light the vessel or object being towed or at least indicate the presence of [*such/ unlighted*] vessel or object.

      (i)   Notwithstanding paragraph (c), on the Western Rivers (except below the Huey P. Long Bridge on the Mississippi River) and on waters specified by the Secretary, a power-driven vessel when pushing ahead or towing alongside, except as paragraph (b) applies, shall exhibit: **INLD**

      (i)   sidelights; and **INLD**

      (ii)   two towing lights in a vertical line. **INLD**

(i/j)   Where from any sufficient cause it is impracticable for a vessel not normally engaged in towing operations to display the lights prescribed in paragraph (a), (c) *or (i)* **INLD** of this Rule, such vessel shall not be required to exhibit those lights when engaged in towing another vessel in distress or otherwise in need of assistance. All possible measures shall be taken to indicate the nature of the relationship between the towing vessel and the vessel being towed as authorized by Rule 36 **(Signaling to Attract Attention),** in particular by illuminating the [*towline/tow*].

This section (i/j) of Rule 24 allows vessels, such as recreational boats, to tow without the need to mount or light the towing or special flashing lights called for here. The only requirement is that some means (light and/or sound) be employed to attract attention to the fact that you are towing or being towed—The Editors.

Rule 24a
Power-driven vessel towing astern - towing vessel less than 50 meters (164 ft.) in length; length of tow exceeds 200 meters (656.2 ft.).

Rule 24a
Power-driven vessel towing astern - towing vessel less than 50 meters (164 ft.) in length; length of tow 200 meters (656.2 ft.) or less.

Rule 24b
Composite unit underway.

Rule 24b
Composite unit underway - less than 50 meters (164 ft.) in length.

Rule 24c
Power-driven vessel pushing ahead or towing alongside - towing vessel less than 50 meters (164 ft.) in length. International

Rule 24c
Power-driven vessel pushing ahead or towing alongside - towing vessel less than 50 meters (164 ft.) in length. Inland

Rule 24d
Power-driven vessel towing astern - length of tow 200 meters (656.2 ft.) or less. The after masthead light is optional for vessel less than 50 meters (164 ft.) in length.

Rule 24d
Power-driven vessel towing astern - length of tow 200 meters (656.2 ft.) or less. When masthead lights for towing or pushing are exhibited aft, a forward masthead light is required.

Rule 24e
Vessel or object being towed - length of tow exceeds 200 meters (656.2 ft.).

Rule 24e
Vessel being towed - length of tow 200 meters (656.2 ft.) or less.

Rule 24f
Vessel being pushed ahead, not being part of a composite unit. International

Rule 24f
Vessel being towed alongside. International

Rule 24f
Vessel being pushed ahead, not being part of a composite unit. Inland

Rule 24f
Vessel being towed alongside. Inland

Rule 24g
Dracone being towed. International

Rule 24i
Power-driven vessel pushing ahead on Western Rivers. (above the Huey P. Long Bridge on the Mississippi River) Inland

RULE 25. SAILING VESSELS UNDERWAY AND VESSELS UNDER OARS

Under both International and Inland Rules a sailboat less than 65.6 ft. (20 meters) and under sail may exhibit running lights at night (see Rule 20) in any one of three different configurations. First, there are the familiar red and green sidelights plus a white sternlight mounted on the hull or in the rigging. Then there's the combination red/green/white light mounted at the top of the mast, without sidelights and sternlight. And finally there is the familiar running light pattern plus red and green all-round lights arranged vertically at the mast top. Sailors who cruise in waters where large ships might be encountered often select options two and three. Mast top lights are usually more visible from the bridge of a ship than sidelights normally mounted on sailboats nearer the water. As stated in section (e), a sailboat under both sail and power must display an inverted black cone as a day signal when sailing under International Rules. When under Inland Rules, sailboats less than 39.4 ft. (12 meters) are not required to hoist such a shape. Of course any sailboat under power must conform to the power-driven requirements stated in Rule 23.

Rule 25 also addresses the lights needed for smaller boats such as a dinghy under oars. Here, a light such as a flashlight should be readily at hand. Rule 23(c) covers most dinghies with outboards used by recreational boaters—The Editors.

(a)   A sailing vessel underway shall exhibit:

(i)   sidelights;

(ii) a sternlight.

(b)   In a sailing vessel of less than 20 meters **(39.4 ft.)** in length the lights prescribed in paragraph (a) of this Rule may be combined in one lantern carried at or near the top of the mast where it can best be seen.

(c)   A sailing vessel underway may, in addition to the lights prescribed in paragraph (a) of this Rule, exhibit at or near the top of the mast, where they can best be seen, two all-round lights in a vertical line, the upper being red and the lower green, but these lights shall not be exhibited in conjunction with the combined lantern permitted by paragraph (b) of this Rule.

Rule 25a
Sailing vessel underway.

Rule 25b
Sailing vessel underway - less than 20 meters (65.6 ft.) in length.

Rule 25c
Sailing vessel underway.

Rule 25d
Sailing vessel underway - less than 7 meters (23 ft.) in length.

Rule 25d
Vessel under oars.

Rule 25e
Vessel processing under sail when also being propelled by machinery. Same for Inland except that a vessel of less than 12 meters (39.4 ft.) in length is not required to exhibit the dayshape.

(d)   (i)   A sailing vessel of less than 7 meters **(23 ft.)** in length shall, if practicable, exhibit the lights prescribed in paragraph (a) or (b) of this Rule, but if she does not, she shall have ready at hand an electric torch or lighted lantern showing a white light which shall be exhibited in sufficient time to prevent collision.

        (ii)   A vessel under oars may exhibit the lights prescribed in this rule for sailing vessels, but if she does not, she shall have ready at hand an electric torch or lighted lantern showing a white light which shall be exhibited in sufficient time to prevent collision.

(e)   A vessel proceeding under sail when also being propelled by machinery shall exhibit forward where it can best be seen a conical shape, apex downwards. *A vessel of less than 12 meters* **(39.4 ft.)** *in length is not required to exhibit this shape, but may do so.* **INLD**

RULE 26. FISHING VESSELS

Rules 26 through 31 deal with running lights and shapes not normally encountered by the average recreational boater. There are, however, times when he may be operating offshore at night and see different light configurations. These may well be confusing. It is important to have handy a copy of the Rules with diagrams. According to the Pilot Rules in Annex V, such a manual must be aboard all vessels 39.4 ft. (12 meters) or longer in length. Remember, too, that the Rules for fishermen "trawling" do not apply to recreational sportfishermen who are trolling [Rule 3(d)] —The Editors.

(a)   A vessel engaged in fishing, whether underway or at anchor, shall exhibit only the lights and shapes prescribed in this Rule.

(b)   A vessel when engaged in trawling, by which is meant the dragging through the water of a dredge net or other apparatus used as a fishing appliance, shall exhibit:

      (i)   two all-round lights in a vertical line, the upper being green and the lower white, or a shape consisting of two cones with their apexes together in a vertical line one above the other;

      (ii)   a masthead light abaft of and higher than the all-round green light; a vessel of less than 50 meters **(164 ft.)** in length shall not be obliged to exhibit such a light but may do so;

      (iii) when making way through the water, in addition to the lights prescribed in this paragraph, sidelights and a sternlight.

(c)   A vessel engaged in fishing, other than trawling, shall exhibit:

      (i)   two all-round lights in a vertical line, the upper being red and the lower white, or a shape consisting of two cones with their apexes together in a vertical line one above the other;

      (ii)   when there is outlying gear extending more than 150 meters **(492.1 ft.)** horizontally from the vessel, an all-round white light or a cone apex upwards in the direction of the gear;

      (iii) when making way through the water, in addition to the lights prescribed in this paragraph, sidelights and a sternlight.

(d)   The additional signals described in Annex II to these Rules apply to a vessel engaged in fishing in close proximity to other vessels engaged in fishing.

(e)   A vessel when not engaged in fishing shall not exhibit the lights or shapes prescribed in this Rule, but only those prescribed for a vessel of her length.

Rule 26b
Vessel engaged in trawling-not making way.

Rule 26b
Vessel engaged in trawling - not making way; vessel less than 50 meters (164 ft.) in length.

Rule 26b
Vessel engaged in trawling - making way; vessel less than 50 meters (164 ft.) in length.

Rule 26b
Vessel engaged in trawling - making way.

When there is outlying gear extending more than 150 meters horizontally from the vessel, an all-round white light or a cone apex upwards in the direction of the gear.

Rule 26c
Vessel engaged in fishing other than trawling - making way.

When there is outlying gear extending more than 150 meters horizontally from the vessel, an all-round white light or a cone apex upwards in the direction of the gear.

Rule 26c
Vessel engaged in fishing other than trawling - not making way.

RULE 27. VESSELS NOT UNDER COMMAND OR RESTRICTED IN THEIR ABILITY TO MANEUVER

Even though this Rule starts with a vessel not under command, it deals mainly with the lights and shapes that vessels should display if somehow they are restricted in their ability to maneuver. This includes dredges, heavy tows, minesweepers and, of special concern to recreational boaters, dive boats. All boats under 39.4 ft. (20 meters) in length need not display the lights and shapes shown here except for those vessels involved with dive operations. The official dive flag is noted under Rule 27(e). It's the blue and white swallow-tailed code flag "A". This is the only flag recognized by both the Inland and International Rules. Use of the unofficial red flag with white diagonal stripe is most often used on lakes and ponds governed by local or state ordinances. Sometimes it marks the location of the actual diver, sometimes the boat used by the diver. It's best to be aware of both flags and their meanings —The Editors.

(a)   A vessel not under command shall exhibit:

    (i)   two all-round red lights in a vertical line where they can best be seen;

    (ii)   two balls or similar shapes in a vertical line where they can best be seen;

    (iii) when making way through the water, in addition to the lights prescribed in this paragraph, sidelights and a sternlight.

(b)   A vessel restricted in her ability to maneuver, except a vessel engaged in mineclearance operations, shall exhibit:

    (i)   three all-round lights in a vertical line where they can best be seen. The highest and lowest of these lights shall be red and the middle light shall be white;

    (ii)   three shapes in a vertical line where they can best be seen. The highest and lowest of these shapes shall be balls and the middle one a diamond.

(iii) when making way through the water, [a masthead light or lights/masthead lights], sidelights and a stern light in addition to the lights prescribed in subparagraph (b)(i);

(iv) when at anchor, in addition to the lights or shapes prescribed in subparagraphs (b)(i) and (b)(ii), the light, lights or shapes prescribed in Rule 30.

(c) A power-driven vessel engaged in a towing operation such as severely restricts the towing vessel and her tow in their ability to deviate from their course shall, in addition to the lights or shapes prescribed in [*Rule 24(a) / subparagraph (b)(i) and (ii) of this Rule*], exhibit the lights or shape prescribed in [*subparagraph (b)(i) and (ii) of this Rule / Rule 24*].

(d) A vessel engaged in dredging or underwater operations, when restricted in her ability to maneuver, shall exhibit the lights and shapes prescribed in subparagraphs (b)(i), (ii) and (iii) of this Rule and shall in addition when an obstruction exists, exhibit:

(i) two all-round red lights or two balls in a vertical line to indicate the side on which the obstruction exists;

(ii) two all-round green lights or two diamonds in a vertical line to indicate the side on which another vessel may pass;

(iii) when at anchor, the lights or shapes prescribed in this paragraph instead of the lights or shapes prescribed in Rule 30, *for anchored vessels.* **INLD**

(e) Whenever the size of a vessel engaged in diving operations makes it impracticable to exhibit all lights and shapes prescribed in paragraph (d) of this Rule, the following shall be exhibited:

(i) Three all-round lights in a vertical line where they can best be seen. The highest and lowest of these lights shall be red and the middle light shall be white;

(ii) a rigid replica of the International Code flag "A" not less than 1 meter **(3.3 ft.)** in height. Measures shall be taken to ensure its all-round visibility.

(f) A vessel engaged in mineclearance operations shall, in addition to the lights prescribed for a power-driven vessel in Rule 23 or to the lights or shape prescribed for a vessel at anchor in Rule 30 as appropriate, exhibit three all-round green lights or three balls. One of these lights or shapes shall be exhibited near the foremast head and one at each end of the fore yard. These lights or shapes indicate that it is dangerous for another vessel to approach within 1000 meters **(3,280.8 ft.)** of the mineclearance vessel.

(g) Vessels of less than 12 meters **(39.4 ft.)** in length, except those engaged in diving operations, shall not be required to exhibit the lights prescribed in this Rule.

(h) The signals prescribed in this Rule are not signals of vessels in distress and requiring assistance. Such signals are contained in Annex IV to these [*Regulations / Rules*].

Rule 27a
Vessel not under command-not making way.

Rule 27a
Vessel not under command-making way.

Rule 27b
Vessel restricted in her ability to maneuver - making way; vessel less than 50 meters (164 ft.) in length.

Rule 27b
Vessel restricted in her ability to maneuver - at anchor; vessel less than 50 meters (164 ft.) in length.

Rule 27c
Vessel engaged in towing operation which severely restricts towing vessel and her tow in their ability to deviate from their course - length of tow does not exceed 200 meters (656.2 ft.); towing vessel less than 50 meters (164 ft.) in length.

Rule 27d
Vessel engaged in dredging or underwater operations when restricted in ability to maneuver - making way with an obstruction on the starboard side.

Rule 27d
Vessel engaged in dredging or underwater operations when restricted in ability to maneuver - not making way with an obstruction on the starboard side.

Rule 27e
Vessel engaged in diving operations.

Rule 27e
Vessel engaged in diving operations.

Rule 27f
**Vessel engaged in mineclearance opera-
tions - vessel less than 50 meters (164
ft.) in length.**

Rule 27f
**Vessel engaged in mineclearance
operations.**

RULE 28. CONSTRAINED BY DRAFT (INTL ONLY) //

A vessel constrained by her draft (referred to as a COD) may, in addition to the lights prescribed for power-driven vessels in Rule 23, exhibit where they can best be seen three all–round red lights in a vertical line, or a cylinder.

Rule 28
Vessel constrained by her draft.

RULE 29. PILOT VESSELS //

(a)   A vessel engaged on pilotage duty shall exhibit:

    (i)   at or near the masthead, two all–round lights in a vertical line, the upper being white and the lower red;

    (ii)   when underway, in addition, sidelights and a stern light;

    (iii)   when at anchor, in addition to the lights prescribed in subparagraph (i), the light, lights, or shape prescribed in Rule 30 for [vessels at anchor / anchored vessels].

(b)   A pilot vessel when not engaged on pilotage duty shall
        exhibit the lights or shapes prescribed for a similar vessel of
        her length.

Rule 29a
Vessel engaged on pilotage duty -under-way.

Rule 29a
Vessel engaged on pilotage duty - at anchor; vessel less than 50 meters (164 ft.) in length.

RULE 30/31. ANCHORED VESSELS AND VESSELS AGROUND/SEAPLANES

Rule 30

(a)   A vessel at anchor shall exhibit where it can best be seen:

    (i)   in the fore part, an all-round white light or one ball;

    (ii)   at or near the stern and at a lower level than the light
        prescribed in subparagraph (i), an all-round white
        light.

(b)   A vessel of less than 50 meters **(164 ft.)** in length may
        exhibit an all-round white light where it can best be seen
        instead of the lights prescribed in paragraph (a) of this
        Rule.

Because they are less than 164 ft. in length, most recreational boats should show an all-around white light and a black ball when at anchor. As you'll see in paragraphs (e), (f) and (Inland g), boats under 23 ft. need not use any lights or balls when anchored outside the normal navigation areas, and, under Inland Rules, boats under 65.6 ft. need not sport a light or ball when in a designated area such as a yacht club anchorage. The catch here is in paragraph (f), dealing with groundings. When a boat less than 164 ft. but more than 39.4 ft. is aground it needs to show two all-round red lights, one all-round white light and three black balls in a vertical line [Rule 30 (b) and (d)]. Few if any recreational boats 40 ft. or more carry two red lights and three black balls that can be rigged vertically if the boat becomes grounded. But it's in the Rules. No lights or balls are required aboard a boat less than 39.4 ft. when aground—The Editors.

(c)   A vessel at anchor may, and a vessel of 100 meters **(328.1 ft.)** and more in length shall, also use the available working or equivalent lights to illuminate her decks.

(d)   A vessel aground shall exhibit the lights prescribed in paragraph (a) or (b) of this Rule and in addition, *if practicable* **INLD**, where they can best be seen:

(i)   two all-round red lights in a vertical line;

(ii)   three balls in a vertical line.

(e)   A vessel of less than 7 meters **(23 ft.)** in length, when at anchor, not in or near a narrow channel, fairway or where other vessels normally navigate, shall not be required to exhibit the lights or anchorage shape prescribed in paragraphs (a) and (b) of this Rule.

(f)   A vessel of less than 12 meters **(39.4 ft.)** in length, when aground, shall not be required to exhibit the lights or shapes prescribed in subparagraphs (d)(i) and (ii) of this Rule.

Rule 30a
Vessel at anchor with deck illumination.

Rule 30b
Vessel at anchor - less than 50 meters (164 ft.) in length.

Rule 30d
Vessel aground.

Rule 30d
Vessel aground - less than 50 meters (164 ft.) in length (but more than 39.4 ft.).

(g)   *A vessel of less than 20 meters* **(65.6 ft.)** *in length, when at anchor in a special anchorage area designated by the Secretary, shall not be required to exhibit the anchor lights and shapes required by this Rule.* **INLD**

Rule 31

Where it is impracticable for a seaplane or a *WIG craft* **INTL** (effective 11/29/03) to exhibit lights or shapes of the characteristics or in the positions prescribed in the Rules of this Part she shall exhibit lights and shapes as closely similar in characteristics and position as is possible.

PART D, SOUND AND LIGHT SIGNALS

Rules 32-37

This is one of the most important sections because it covers the sound signals that all vessels including recreational boats use to signify maneuvers, danger, and distress. Covered too are those signals used in fog by both powerboats and sailboats. Though the Rules stipulate that light signals may be used as well as sound, few if any recreational boats use lights to indicate maneuvers. Distress signals, however, may entail the use of flares or flashing lights as described in Rules 36 and 37—The Editors.

RULE 32/33. DEFINITIONS/ EQUIPMENT FOR SOUND SIGNALS

Rule 32

(a) The word "whistle" means any sound signaling appliance capable of producing the prescribed blasts and which complies with the specifications in Annex III to these [*Regulations* **INTL**/*Rules* **INLD**].

The term "whistle" should not be mistaken for the familiar police whistle. As stated in 32(a) it means any sound-producing device, from a portable air horn to the robust boomers of the QE2. For recreational boaters what's important here is to recognize the different sounds that are made by vessels of varying lengths. These are detailed in Annex III. When operating in fog or other restricted visibility you will be able to roughly determine the size of the unseen vessel by listening for the tone or pitch of its horn. A vessel less than 246.1 ft. (75 meters) sounds a horn with a higher frequency, while a vessel longer than 246.1 ft. but less than 656.2 ft. (200 meters) carries a lower sounding horn. A vessel more than 656.2 ft. uses one even lower. When you hear it you won't mistake the booming, deep-throated sound. Annex III also details the specs for bells and gongs required aboard different size vessels.

    This paragraph also defines the duration of a short blast and a prolonged blast. These definitions are important when maneuvering and operating in fog—The Editors.

(b)   The term "short blast" means a blast of about one second's duration.

(c)   The term "prolonged blast" means a blast of from four to six seconds' duration.

Rule 33

(a)   A vessel of 12 meters **(39.4 ft.)** or more in length shall be provided with a whistle *and a bell* **INLD**, *a vessel of 20 meters* **(65.6 ft.)** *or more in length shall be provided with a bell in addition to a whistle* **INTL** (effective 11/29/03), and a vessel of 100 meters **(328.1 ft.)** or more in length shall, in addition, be provided with a gong, the tone and sound of which cannot be confused with that of the bell. The whistle, bell and gong shall comply with the specifications in Annex III to these *Regulations* **INTL** (effective 11/29/03)/ Rules. The bell or gong or both may be replaced by other equipment having the same respective sound characteristics, provided that manual sounding of the prescribed signals shall always be possible.

The Inland text does not change but retains the need for a vessel 39.4 ft. or more in length to have a bell. The change to the International Rules (COLREGS) becomes effective on November 29, 2003. Basically it eliminates the original bell requirement for vessels from 39.4 ft. to 65.6 ft. Such boats need carry only a whistle, but one specified in Annex III. As noted in 33(b) a vessel under 39.4 ft. need carry only some sound-producing device, not necessarily one with the specifications required under Annex III
—The Editors.

(b)   A vessel of less than 12 meters **(39.4 ft.)** in length shall not be obliged to carry the sound signaling appliances prescribed in paragraph (a) of this Rule but if she does not, she shall be provided with some other means of making an efficient signal.

RULE 34. MANEUVERING AND WARNING SIGNALS //

For recreational boaters this is by far one of the most important Rules. It details the maneuvering signals to be used in both International and Inland waters when power-driven vessels are within sight of one another. The major difference between the two is evident right in paragraph (a). Under International Rules a signal indicating movement to port or starboard is an action signal "I am altering...." It requires no response unless danger exists. Under Inland Rules, though the wording is confusingly different, the result can be the same. Here "intent" rather than action is expressed: "I intend to leave you on my ... side." A response is required. It can be in kind or can be the danger signal. In both International and Inland Rules three short blasts is an action signal signifying astern propulsion even if the vessel is not moving astern as yet.

Differences appear again in (c) when vessels are overtaking. Here "intent" rather than "action" is indicated but the actual expression of "intent" and the signals used are different. Under International Rules intent is indicated by sounding two prolonged blasts followed by one or two shorts blasts depending on the side with which the overtaken vessel is to be passed. Under Inland Rules only a short or prolonged blast will be used to indicate side. This also differs from (a) as to meaning: "I intend to overtake you on your... side." The vessel being overtaken will respond in kind under Inland Rules if it agrees or signal danger if not. Under International Rules the response, if in agreement, will be one pro-longed, one short, one prolonged, one short—the Morse Code letter "C" meaning "Yes". If not in agreement, the danger signal will be sounded.

Obviously, many recreational skippers find all of this very con-fusing and set up their own system. One short blast, for example, will accompany any movement of the bow to starboard; two to port.

Radio contact is also possible. Explicitly authorized under Inland Rules, communicating by VHF radio is especially helpful when recreational boats encounter commercial traffic in crowded waters such as the Intracoastal Waterway. Here a simplified system has come into use. "I'll meet you on one, Cap," can mean a port-to-port pass when meeting head on. When overtaking, it can also mean your-port-to-his-starboard pass. "On two" means a starboard-to-starboard pass or starboard-to-port overtaking.

In both Rules, vessels approaching a bend or leaving a slip will sound one prolonged blast. And of course both Rules call for five or more short and rapid blasts to indicate DANGER
—The Editors.

INTERNATIONAL

(a) When vessels are in sight of one another, a power-driven vessel underway, when maneuvering as authorized or required by these Rules, shall indicate that maneuver by the following signals on her whistle:

• one short blast to mean "I am altering my course to starboard";
• two short blasts to mean "I am altering my course to port";
• three short blasts to mean "I am operating astern propulsion".

INLAND

(a) When power-driven vessels are in sight of one another and meeting or crossing at a distance within half a mile of each other, each vessel underway, when maneuvering as authorized or required by these Rules:

(i) shall indicate that maneuver by the following signals on her whistle:
• one short blast to mean "I intend to leave you on my port side";
• two short blasts to mean "I intend to leave you on my starboard side";
• three short blasts to mean "I am operating astern propulsion".

(ii) upon hearing the one or two blast signal of the other shall, if in agreement, sound the same whistle signal and take the steps necessary to effect a safe passing. If, however, from any cause, the vessel doubts the safety of the proposed maneuver, she shall sound the danger signal specified in paragraph (d) of this Rule and each vessel shall take appropriate precautionary action until a safe passing agreement is made.

(b) Any vessel may supplement the whistle signals prescribed in paragraph (a) of this Rule by light signals, repeated as appropriate, while the maneuver is being carried out:

(i) these signals shall have the following significance:
• one flash to mean "I am altering my course to starboard";
• two flashes to mean "I am altering my course to port";
• three flashes to mean "I am operating astern propulsion".

(ii) the duration of each flash shall be about one second, the interval between flashes shall be about one second, and the interval between successive signals shall not be less than ten seconds.

(iii) the light used for this signal shall, if fitted, be an all-round white light, visible at a minimum range of 5 miles, and shall comply with the provisions of Annex I to these Regulations.

(b) Any vessel may supplement the whistle signals prescribed in paragraph (a) of this Rule by light signals:

(i) these signals shall have the following significance:
• one flash to mean "I intend to leave you on my port side";
• two flashes to mean "I intend to leave you on my starboard side";
• three flashes to mean "I am operating astern propulsion".

(ii) the duration of each flash shall be about one second;

(iii) the light used for this signal shall, if fitted, be an all-round white or yellow light, visible at a minimum range of 2 miles, synchronized with the whistle, and shall comply with the provisions of Annex I to these Rules.

(c) When in sight of one another in a narrow channel or fairway:

(i) a vessel intending to overtake another shall in compliance with Rule 9(e)(i) indicate her intention by the following signals on her whistle:
• two prolonged blasts followed by one short blast to mean "I intend to overtake you on your starboard side";
• two prolonged by two prolonged blasts followed by two short blasts to mean "I intend to overtake you on your port side".

(ii) the vessel about to be overtaken when acting in accordance with 9(e)(i) shall indicate her agreement by the following signal on her whistle:
• one prolonged, one short,
• one prolonged and one short blast, in that order.

(c) When in sight of one another :

(i) a power-driven vessel intending to overtake another power-driven vessel shall indicate her intention by the following signals on her whistle:
• one short blast to mean "I intend to overtake you on your starboard side";
• two short blasts to mean "I intend to overtake you on your port side".

(ii) the power-driven vessel about to be overtaken shall, if in agreement, sound a similar signal. If in doubt she shall sound the danger signal prescribed in paragraph (d).

(d)   When vessels in sight of one another are approaching each other and from any cause either vessel fails to understand the intentions or actions of the other, or is in doubt whether sufficient action is being taken by the other to avoid collision, the vessel in doubt shall immediately indicate such doubt by giving at least five short and rapid blasts on the whistle. *Such* **INTL** *This* **INLD** signal may be supplemented by at least five short and rapid flashes.

(e)   A vessel nearing a bend or an area of a channel or fairway where other vessels may be obscured by an intervening obstruction shall sound one prolonged blast. Such signal shall be answered with a prolonged blast by any approaching vessel that may be within hearing around the bend or behind the intervening obstruction.

(f)   If whistles are fitted on a vessel at a distance apart of more than 100 meters **(328.1 ft.),** one whistle only shall be used for giving maneuvering and warning signals.

(g)   *When a power-driven vessel is leaving a dock or berth, she shall sound one prolonged blast.* **INLD**

(h)   *A vessel that reaches agreement with another vessel in a head-on, crossing, or overtaking situation, as for example, by using the radiotelephone as prescribed by the Vessel Bridge-to-Bridge Radiotelephone Act (85 Stat. 164; 33 U.S.C. 1201 et seq.), is not obliged to sound the whistle signals prescribed by this Rule, but may do so. If agreement is not reached, then whistle signals shall be exchanged in a timely manner and shall prevail.* **INLD**

RULE 35. SOUND SIGNALS IN RESTRICTED VISIBILITY

Though restricted visibility is defined to include rain, snow, and sand storms, most recreational boaters will find themselves in fog. Therefore it's important to recognize the fog signals of other types of vessels, especially those signals prescribed for power-boats in paragraph (a) and for sailboats in paragraph (c). These are the signals most used by recreational boaters—The Editors.

In or near an area of restricted visibility, whether by day or night the signals prescribed in this Rule shall be used as follows:

(a)   A power-driven vessel making way through the water shall sound at intervals of not more than 2 minutes one prolonged blast.

(b)   A power-driven vessel underway but stopped and making no way through the water shall sound at intervals of no more than 2 minutes two prolonged blasts in succession with an interval of about 2 seconds between them.

(c)   A vessel not under command, a vessel restricted in her ability to maneuver *whether underway or at anchor* **INLD**, *a vessel constrained by her draft* **INTL** , a sailing vessel, a vessel engaged in fishing *whether underway or at anchor* **INLD** and a vessel engaged in towing or pushing another vessel shall, instead of the signals prescribed in paragraph (a) or (b) of this Rule, sound at intervals of not more than 2 minutes three blasts in succession, namely one prolonged followed by two short blasts.

(d)   *A vessel engaged in fishing, when at anchor, and a vessel restrict ed in her ability to maneuver when carrying out her work at anchor, shall instead of the signals prescribed in paragraph (g) of this Rule sound the signal prescribed in paragraph (c) of this Rule.* **INTL**

(e/d)   A vessel towed or if more than one vessel is towed the last vessel of the tow, if manned, shall at intervals of not more than 2 minutes sound four blasts in succession, namely one prolonged followed by three short blasts. When practicable, this signal shall be made immediately after the signal made by the towing vessel.

(f/e)   When a pushing vessel and a vessel being pushed ahead are rigidly connected in a composite unit they shall be regarded as a power-driven vessel and shall give the signals prescribed in paragraphs (a) or (b) of this Rule.

(g/f)   A vessel at anchor shall at intervals of not more than 1 minute ring the bell rapidly for ten seconds. In a vessel 100 meters **(328.1 ft.)** or more in length the bell shall be sounded in the forepart of the vessel and immediately after the ringing of the bell the gong shall be sounded rapidly for about 5 seconds in the after part of the vessel. A vessel at anchor may in addition sound three blasts in succession, namely one short, one long and one short blast, to give warning of her position and of the possibility of collision to an approaching vessel.

(h/g) A vessel aground shall give the bell signal and if required the gong signal prescribed in paragraph [(g) / (f)] of this Rule and shall, in addition, give three separate and distinct strokes on the bell immediately before and after the rapid ringing of the bell. A vessel aground may in addition sound an appropriate whistle signal.

(i/-) *A vessel of 12 meters* **(39.4 ft.)** *or more but less than 20 meters* **(65.6 ft.)** *in length shall not be obliged to give the bell signals prescribed in paragraphs (g) and (h) of this Rule. However, if she does not, she shall make some other efficient sound signal at intevals of not more than 2 minutes.* **INTL** *(effective 11/29/03)*

(j/h) *A vessel of less than 12 meters* **(39.4 ft.)** *in length shall not be obliged to give the above mentioned signals but, if she does not, shall make some other efficient sound signal at intervals of not more than 2 minutes.* **INLD**

(k/i) A pilotage vessel when engaged on pilotage duty may in addition to the signals prescribed in paragraph (a), (b) or (g)/(f) of this Rule sound an identity signal consisting of four short blasts.

(j) *The following vessels shall not be required to sound signals as prescribed in paragraph (f) of this Rule when anchored in a special anchorage area designated by the Secretary:*

   (ii)   a vessel of less than 20 meters **(65.6 ft.)** *in length; and*

   (iii) a barge, canal boat boat, scow, or other nondescript craft. **INLD**

Rule 36

If necessary to attract the attention of another vessel, any vessel may make light or sound signals that cannot be mistaken for any signal authorized elsewhere in these Rules, or may direct the beam of her searchlight in the direction of the danger, in such a way as not to embarrass any vessel. Any light to attract the attention of another vessel shall be such that it cannot be mistaken for any aid to navigation. For the purpose of this Rule the use of high intensity intermittent or revolving lights, such as strobe lights, shall be avoided. **INTL**

Rule 37
Distress Signals 72
COLREGS
The distress signals for inland waters are the same as those displayed here with the addition of a high intensity white light.

Rule 37-Inland only
A high intensity white light flashing at regular intervals from 50 to 70 timeer minute.

Rule 37

When a vessel is in distress and requires assistance she shall use or exhibit the signals described in Annex IV to these Regulations.

Though not called for in the Rules, state and federal laws establish certain requirements to carry Visual Distress Signals (VDSs) aboard recreational boats. These regulations call for both day and night signals. These signals can be both pyrotechnic (such as red flares) and non-pyrotechnic (such as smoke signals). Check local laws for the number and type of approved signals. Not all the sight or sound signals authorized here to attract attention fulfill the VDS requirements—The Editors.

PART E, EXEMPTIONS

RULE 38. EXEMPTIONS (INTERNATIONAL)

Any vessel (or class of vessel) provided that she complies with the requirements of the International Regulations for the Preventing of Collisions at Sea, 1960, the keel of which is laid or is at a corresponding stage of construction before the entry into force of these Regulations may be exempted from compliance therewith as follows:

(a)   The installation of lights with ranges prescribed in Rule 22, until four years after the date of entry into force of these regulations.

(b)   The installation of lights with color specifications as prescribed in Section 7 of Annex I to these Regulations, until four years after the entry into force of these Regulations.

(c)   The repositioning of lights as a result of conversion from Imperial to metric units and rounding off measurement figures, permanent exemption.

(d)   (i)   The repositioning of masthead lights on vessels of less than 150 meters **(492.1 ft.)** in length, resulting from the prescriptions of Section 3 (a) of Annex I to these regulations, permanent exemption.

      (ii) The repositioning of masthead lights on vessels of 150 meters **(492.1 ft.)** or more in length, resulting from the prescriptions of Section 3 (a) of Annex I to these regulations, until 9 years after the date of entry into force of these Regulations.

(e)   The repositioning of masthead lights resulting from the prescriptions of Section 2(b) of Annex I to these Regulations, until 9 years after the date of entry into force of these Regulations.

(f)   The repositioning of sidelights resulting from the prescriptions of Section 2(g) and 3(b) of Annex I to these Regulations, until 9 years after the date of entry into force of these Regulations.

(g)   The requirements for sound signal appliances prescribed in Annex III to these Regulations, until 9 years after the date of entry into force of these Regulations.

(h)   The repositioning of all-round lights resulting from the prescription of Section 9(b) of Annex I to these Regulations, permanent exemption.

RULE 38. EXEMPTIONS (INLAND)

Any vessel or class of vessels, the keel of which is laid or which is at a corresponding stage of construction before December 24, 1980, provided that she complies with the requirements of –

(a)   The Act of June 7, 1897 (30 Stat. 96), as amended (33 U.S.C. 154-232) for vessels navigating the waters subject to that statute;

(b)   Section 4233 of the Revised Statutes (33 U.S.C. 301-356) for vessels navigating the waters subject to that statute;

(c)   The Act of February 8, 1895 (28 Stat. 645), as amended (33 U.S.C. 241-295) for vessels navigating the waters subject to that statute; or

(d)   Sections 3, 4, and 5 of the Act of April 25, 1940 (54 Stat. 163), as amended (46 U.S.C. 526 b, c, and d) for motorboats navigating the waters subject to that statute; shall be exempted from compliance with the technical Annexes to these Rules as follows:

(i)   The installation of lights with ranges prescribed in Rule 22, until 4 years after the effective date of these Rules, except that vessels of less than 20 meters **(65.6 ft.)** in length are permanently exempt;

(ii) The installation of lights with color specifications as prescribed in Section 7 of Annex I to these Rules, until 4 years after the effective date of these Rules, except that vessels of less than 20 meters **(65.6 ft.)** in length are permanently exempt;

(iii) The repositioning of lights as a result of a conversion to metric units and rounding off of measurement figures, are permanently exempt; and.

(iv) The horizontal repositioning of masthead lights prescribed by Annex I to these Rules:

(1)   on vessels of less than 150 meters **(492.1 ft.)** in length, permanent exemption.

(2)   on vessels of 150 meters **(492.1 ft.)** or more in length, until 9 years after the effective date of these Rules.

(v)   The restructuring or repositioning of all lights to meet the prescriptions of Annex I to these Rules, until 9 years after the effective date of these Rules;

(vi) Power-driven vessels of 12 meters **(39.4 ft.)** or more but less than 20 meters **(65.6 ft.)** in length are permanently exempt from the provisions of Rule 23(a)(i) and 23(a)(iv) provided that, in place of these lights, the vessel exhibits a white light aft visible all round the horizon **(See Rule 23(a)(ii) for COMMENTS);** and

(vii) The requirements for sound signal appliances prescribed in Annex III to these Rules, until 9 years after the effective date of these Rules.

ANNEXES AND OTHER REGULATIONS

The following five Annexes to the Rules detail many of the technical specifications and positioning requirements called for in Rules 1 through 38. Annexes I, II, and III deal with lights, shapes, and sounds mandated on vessels and ships (for the most part) longer than 65.6 ft. (20 meters). Though the specs detailed in some Annex sections refer to vessels less than 65.6 ft., they are generally already fulfilled by the boat manufacturer and need only be checked by a recreational boat owner.

Annexes IV and V are of specific interest to operators of recreational boats. These deal with recognized distress signals and with lights used on law enforcement vessels and moored barges in inland waters.

The organization of the Annexes differs somewhat from the combined form found in the actual Rules. Because there are so many differences between the two, the International and Inland Annexes are placed on facing pages with International on the left and Inland on the right. In the case of Annex V there are only Inland and no International entries; therefore this Piloting section will appear on a single page.

Following the Annexes are eight regulations that are of interest to boaters. Of most interest is the section detailing the position of the demarcation lines. It's this line that separates the waters between International and Inland Rules. International Rules apply on waters to seaward of the line, Inland Rules to those waters between the shore and the line.

The Penalties section is the most important because it deals with three very important aspects of boat operation. First, it details the penalties for negligence in boat operations. Then it lays out the responsibilities and duties of those involved in a maritime accident. This section also exempts from liability those providing assistance when involved in an accident. And, finally, it states a mariner's mandate to assist vessels that are in danger of being lost.

Other sections include Interpretative Rules, Alternative Compliance, Waters Designated by the Secretary, Bridge-to-Bridge Radiotelephone (VHF) Communications, Vessel Traffic Services, and Legal Citations. **This last is of special interest because the Rules and Regulations noted in this book are not the basis for legal action. Reference to the actual Citations is needed for any legal activity.**

ANNEX I

This section deals with the positioning and technical specifications for shipboard lights and shapes. Practically all recreational boats have running lights correctly positioned and of proper illumination as prescribed within this section. There is little need for pleasure boat skippers to refer to Annex I.

ANNEX II

Additional lights mounted by commercial vessels when fishing in close proximity are listed here.

ANNEX III

Technical data for sound equipment (whistles), including frequencies and ranges, are detailed in this section.

ANNEX IV

This is a very important section for recreational boaters. It lists the recognized distress signals available to a skipper should an emergency require a call for help. It further explains those signals shown in Rule 37.

ANNEX V
Called the Pilot Rules, this Inland-only annex spells out the need for a copy of the Rules aboard all vessels 39.4 ft. (12 meters) in length and longer. It also details the lights used by boats engaged in law enforcement and public safety activities.

INTERPRETATIVE RULES
A more defined explanation of a Composite Unit, plus additional information regarding lights for moored vessels and sidelights for unmanned barges.

COLREGS DEMARCATION LINES
The locations of all the lines that separate International from Inland Rules are listed here. You should check this section to find where the lines that are in your boating waters are located.

PENALTY PROVISIONS
This is a must-read section because it defines your responsibilities when operating a boat, when involved in an accident, and when you come across a vessel in danger of being lost.

ALTERNATIVE COMPLIANCE
This regulation allows some deviation from the light, shape, and sound Rules due to unusual vessel construction.

WATERS SPECIFIED BY THE SECRETARY
Certain sections of Inland Rules 9, 14, 15, and 24 are applicable on the waters listed here, designated by the Secretary of the department in which the U.S. Coast Guard is operating. Formerly, the USCG operated under the Department of Transportation; it now operates under the Department of Homeland Security.

VESSEL BRIDGE-TO-BRIDGE RADIOTELEPHONE REGULATIONS
This act authorizes the use of VHF radio communications for vessel navigation. Rule 34(h) recognizes that such communica-

tions may be used instead of whistle signals to signify maneuvering action or intent.

VESSEL TRAFFIC SERVICES

This part lists the VHF channels and monitoring areas of those eight regions in which vessel traffic systems are established.

LEGAL CITATIONS

Since these Rules, Annexes, and separate sections are not the foundations for legal action, it is necessary to cite the location of the actual laws that apply in this compendium.

—The Editors

33 CFR 84: ANNEX I - INLAND POSITIONING & TECHNICAL DETAILS OF LIGHTS & SHAPES

§84.01. Definition

§84.03. Vertical Positioning and Spacing of Lights

§84.05. Horizontal Positioning and Spacing of Lights

§84.07. Details of location of direction-indicating lights for fishing vessels, dredgers and vessels engaged in underwater operations

§84.09. Screens for Sidelights

§84.11. Shapes

§84.13. Color Specification of Lights

§84.15 Intensity of Lights

§84.17. Horizontal Sectors

§84.19. Vertical Sectors

§84.21. Intensity of Non-Electric Lights

§84.23. Maneuvering Light

§84.24. High Speed Craft

§84.25. Approval [Reserved]

§ 84.01 Definitions

(a) The term "height above the hull" means height above the uppermost continuous deck. This height shall be measured from the position vertically beneath the location of the light.

(b) High-speed craft means a craft capable of maximum speed in meters per second (m/s) equal to or exceeding: $3.7\nabla 0.1667$; where $\nabla =$ displacement corresponding to the design waterline (meters3).

(c) The term "practical cut-off" means, for vessels 20 meters or more in length, 12.5 percent of the minimum luminous intensity (Table 84.15(b)) corresponding to the greatest range of visibility for which the requirements of Annex I are met.

(d) The term "Rule" or "Rules" means the Inland Navigation Rules contained in Sec. 2 of the Inland Navigational Rules Act of 1980 (Pub. L. 96-591, 94 Stat. 3415, 33 U.S.C. 2001, December 24, 1980) as amended.

NOTE to paragraph (b): The same formula expressed in pounds and knots is maximum speed in knots (kts) equal to or exceeding 1.98 (lbs) $3.7s\nabla .1667$; where $\nabla =$ displacement corresponding to design waterline in pounds.

§ 84.03 Vertical positioning and spacing of lights

(a) On a power-driven vessel of 20 meters or more in length the masthead lights shall be placed as follows:

(1) The forward masthead light, or if only one masthead light is carried, then that light, at a height above the hull of not less than 5 meters, and, if the breadth of the vessel exceeds 5 meters, then at a height above the hull not less than such breadth, so however that the light need not be placed at a greater height above the hull than 8 meters;

(2) When two masthead lights are carried the after one shall be at least 2 meters vertically higher than the forward one.

(b) The vertical separation of the masthead lights of power-driven vessels shall be such that in all normal conditions of trim the after light will be seen over and separate from the forward light at a distance of 1000 meters from the stem when viewed from water level.

(c) The masthead light of a power-driven vessel of 12 meters but less than 20 meters in length shall be placed at a height above the gunwale of not less than 2.5 meters.

(d) The masthead light, or the all-round light described in Rule 23(c), of a power-driven vessel of less than 12 meters in length shall be carried at least one meter higher than the sidelights.

(e) One of the two or three masthead lights prescribed for a powerdriven vessel when engaged in towing or pushing another vessel shall be placed in the same position as either the forward masthead light or the after masthead light, provided that the lowest after masthead light shall be at least 2 meters vertically higher than the highest forward masthead light.

(f) (1) The masthead light or lights prescribed in Rule 23(a) shall be so placed as to be above and clear of all other lights and obstructions except as described in paragraph (f)(2) of this section.

(2) When it is impracticable to carry the all-round lights prescribed in Rule 27(b)(i) below the masthead lights, they may be carried above the after masthead light(s) or vertically in between the forward masthead light(s) and after masthead

light(s), provided that in the latter case the requirement of § 84.05(d) shall be complied with.

(g) The sidelights of a power-driven vessel shall be placed at least one meter lower than the forward masthead light. They shall not be so low as to be interfered with by deck lights.

(h) [Reserved]

    (i)   When the Rules prescribe two or three lights to be carried in a vertical line, they shall be spaced as follows:

    (1)   On a vessel of 20 meters in length or more such lights shall be spaced not less than 1 meter apart, and the lowest of these lights shall, except where a towing light is required, be placed at a height of not less than 4 meters above the hull;

    (2)   On a vessel of less than 20 meters in length such lights shall be spaced not less than 1 meter apart and the lowest of these lights shall, except where a towing light is required, be placed at a height of not less than 2 meters above the gunwale;

    (3)   When three lights are carried they shall be equally spaced.

(j) The lower of the two all-round lights prescribed for a vessel when engaged in fishing shall be at a height above the sidelights not less than twice the distance between the two vertical lights.

(k) The forward anchor light prescribed in Rule 30(a)(i), when two are carried, shall not be less than 4.5 meters above the after one. On a vessel of 50 meters or more in length this forward anchor light shall be placed at a height of not less than 6 meters above the hull.

§ 84.05 Horizontal positioning and spacing of lights

(a) Except as specified in paragraph (e) of this section, when two masthead lights are prescribed for a power-driven vessel, the horizontal distance between them must not be less than one quarter of the length of the vessel but need not be more than 50 meters. The forward light shall be placed not more than one half of the length of the vessel from the stem.

(b) On a power-driven vessel of 20 meters or more in length the sidelights shall not be placed in front of the forward masthead lights. They shall be placed at or near the side of the vessel.

(c) When the lights prescribed in Rule 27(b)(i) are placed vertically between the forward masthead light(s) and the after masthead light(s) these all-round lights shall be placed at a horizontal distance of not less than 2 meters from the fore and aft centerline of the vessel in the athwartship direction.

(d) When only one masthead light is prescribed for a power-driven vessel, this light must be exhibited forward of amidships. For a vessel of less than 20 meters in length, the vessel shall exhibit one masthead light as far forward as is practicable.

(e) On power-driven vessels 50 meters but less than 60 meters in length operated on the Western Rivers, and those waters specified in §89.25, the horizontal distance between masthead lights shall not be less than 10 meters.

§ 84.07 Details of location of direction-indicating lights for fishing vessels, dredgers and vessels engaged in underwater operations

(a) The light indicating the direction of the outlying gear from a vessel engaged in fishing as prescribed in Rule 26(c)(ii) shall be placed at a horizontal distance of not less than 2 meters and not more than 6 meters away from the two all-round red and white lights. This light shall be placed not higher than the all-round white light prescribed in Rule 26(c)(i) and not lower than the sidelights.

(b) The lights and shapes on a vessel engaged in dredging or underwater operations to indicate the obstructed side and/or the side on which it is safe to pass, as prescribed in Rule 27(d)(i) and (ii), shall be placed at the maximum practical horizontal distance, but in no case less than 2 meters, from the lights or shapes prescribed in Rule 27(b)(i) and (ii). In no case shall the upper of these lights or shapes be at a greater height than the lower of the three lights or shapes prescribed in Rule 27(b)(i) and (ii).

§ 84.09 Screens

(a) The sidelights of vessels of 20 meters or more in length shall be fitted with mat black inboard screens and meet the requirements of § 84.17. On vessels of less than 20 meters in length, the sidelights, if necessary to meet the requirements of § 84.17, shall be fitted with mat black inboard screens. With a combined lantern, using a single vertical filament and a very narrow division between the green and red sections, external screens need not be fitted.

(b) On power-driven vessels less than 12 meters in length constructed after July 31, 1983, the masthead light, or the all-round light described in Rule 23(c) shall be screened to prevent direct illumination of the vessel forward of the operator's position.

§ 84.11 Shapes

(a) Shapes shall be black and of the following sizes:

(1) A ball shall have a diameter of not less than 0.6 meter;

(2) A cone shall have a base diameter of not less than 0.6 meter and a height equal to its diameter;

(3) A diamond shape shall consist of two cones (as defined in Paragraph (a)(2) of this section) having a common base.

(b) The vertical distance between shapes shall be at least 1.5 meter.

(c) In a vessel of less than 20 meters in length shapes of lesser dimensions but commensurate with the size of the vessel may be used and the distance apart may be correspondingly reduced.

§ 84.13 Color specification of lights

(a) The chromaticity of all navigation lights shall conform to the following standards, which lie within the boundaries of the area of the diagram specified for each color by the International Commission on Illumination (CIE), in the "Colors of Light Signals", which is incorporated by reference. It is Publication CIE No. 2.2. (TC-1.6), 1975, and is available from the Illumination Engineering

Society, 345 East 47th Street, New York, NY 10017. It is also available for inspection at the Office of the Federal Register, Room 8401, 1100 L Street N.W., Washington, D.C. 20408. This incorporation by reference was approved by the Director of the Federal Register.

(b) The boundaries of the area for each color are given by indicating the corner coordinates, which are as follows:

(1) White:

x 0.525 0.525 0.452 0.310 0.310 0.443

y 0.382 0.440 0.440 0.348 0.283 0.382

(2) Green:

x 0.028 0.009 0.300 0.203

y 0.385 0.723 0.511 0.356

(3) Red:

x 0.680 0.660 0.735 0.721

y 0.320 0.320 0.265 0.259

(4) Yellow:

x 0.612 0.618 0.575 0.575

y 0.382 0.382 0.425 0.406

§ 84.15 Intensity of lights

(a) The minimum luminous intensity of lights shall be calculated by using the formula:

$$I = 3.43 \times 10^6 \times T \times D^2 \times K^{-D}$$

where:

I is luminous intensity in candelas under service conditions, T is threshold factor 2×10^{-7} lux, D is range of visibility (luminous range) of the light in nautical miles, K is atmospheric transmissivity. For prescribed lights the value of K shall be 0.8, corresponding to a meteorological visibility of approximately 13 nautical miles.

(b) A selection of figures derived from the formula is given in Table 84.15(b). Table 84.15(b)

Range of visibility (luminous range) of light in nautica luminous miles	Minimum lintensity of light in candelas tor K = 0.8
D	I
1	0.9
2	4.3
3	12
4	27
5	52
6	94

§ 84.17 Horizontal sectors

(a) (1) In the forward direction, sidelights as fitted on the vessel shall show the minimum required intensities. The intensities shall decrease to reach practical cut-off between 1 and 3 degrees outside the prescribed sectors.

(2) For sternlights and masthead lights and at 22.5 degrees abaft the beam for sidelights, the minimum required intensities shall be maintained over the arc of the horizon up to 5 degrees within the limits of the sectors prescribed in Rule 21. From 5 degrees within the prescribed sectors the intensity may decrease by 50 percent up to the prescribed limits; it shall decrease steadily to reach practical cutoff at not more than 5 degrees outside the prescribed sectors.

(b) All-round lights shall be so located as not to be obscured by masts, topmasts or structures within angular sectors of more than 6 degrees, except anchor lights prescribed in Rule 30, which need not be placed at an impracticable height above the hull, and the all-round white light described in Rule 23(d), which may not be obscured at all.

(c) If it is impracticable to comply with paragraph (b) of this section by exhibiting only one all-round light, two all-round lights shall be used suitably positioned or screened to appear, as far as practicable, as one light at a minimum distance of one nautical mile.

NOTE to paragraph (c): Two unscreened all-round lights that are 1.28 meters apart or less will appear as one light to the naked eye at a distance of one nautical mile.

§ 84.19 Vertical sectors

(a) The vertical sectors of electric lights as fitted, with the exception of lights on sailing vessels underway and on unmanned barges, shall ensure that:

(1) At least the required minimum intensity is maintained at all angles from 5 degrees above to 5 degrees below the horizontal;

(2) At least 60 percent of the required minimum intensity is maintained from 7.5 degrees above to 7.5 degrees below the horizontal.

(b) In the case of sailing vessels underway the vertical sectors of electric lights as fitted shall ensure that:

(1) At least the required minimum intensity is maintained at all angles from 5 degrees above to 5 degrees below the horizontal;

(2) At least 50 percent of the required minimum intensity is maintained from 25 degrees above to 25 degrees below the horizontal.

(c) In the case of unmanned barges the minimum required intensity of electric lights as fitted shall be maintained on the horizontal.

(d) In the case of lights other than electric lights these specifications shall be met as closely as possible.

§ 84.21 Intensity of non-electric lights

Non-electric lights shall so far as practicable comply with the minimum intensities, as specified in the Table given in § 84.15.

§ 84.23 Maneuvering light

Notwithstanding the provisions of § 84.03(f), the maneuvering light described in Rule 34(b) shall be placed approximately in the same fore and aft vertical plane as the masthead light or lights and, where practicable, at a minimum height of one-half meter vertically above the forward masthead light, provided that it shall be carried not less than one-half meter vertically above or below the after masthead light. On a vessel where only one masthead light is carried the maneuvering light, if fitted, shall be carried where it can best be seen, not less than one-half meter vertically apart from the masthead light.

§ 84.24 High Speed Craft

(a) The masthead light of high speed craft with a length to breadth ratio of less than 3.0 may be placed at a height related to the breadth lower than that prescribed in Sec. 84.03(a)(1), provided that the base angle of the isosceles triangle formed by the sidelights and masthead light when seen in end elevation is not less than 27 degrees as determined by the formula in paragraph (b) of this section.

(b) The minimum height of masthead light above sidelights is to be determined by the following formula: Tan $27° = x/y$; where Y is the horizontal distance between the sidelights and X is the height of the forward masthead light.

ANNEX I: INTERNATIONAL POSITIONING & TECHNICAL DETAILS OF LIGHTS & SHAPES

1. Definition

The term "height above the hull" means height above the uppermost continuous deck. This height shall be measured from the position vertically beneath the location of the light.

2. Vertical positioning and spacing of lights

(a) On a power-driven vessel of 20 meters or more in length the masthead lights shall be placed as follows:

(i) the forward masthead light, or if only one masthead light is carried, then that light, at a height above the hull of not less than 6 meters, and, if the breadth of the vessel exceeds 6 meters, then at a height above the hull not less than such breadth, so however that the light need not be placed at a greater height above the hull than 12 meters;

(ii) when two masthead lights are carried the after one shall be at least 4.5 meters vertically higher than the forward one.

(b) The vertical separation of masthead lights of power-driven vessels shall be such that in all normal conditions of trim the after light will be seen over and separate from the forward light at a distance of 1000 meters from the stem when viewed from sea level.

(c) The masthead light of a power-driven vessel of 12 meters but less than 20 meters in length shall be placed at a height above the gunwale of not less than 2.5 meters.

(d) A power-driven vessel of less than 12 meters in length may carry the uppermost light at a height of less than 2.5 meters above the gunwale. When, however, a masthead light is carried in addition to sidelights and a sternlight or the all-round light prescribed in rule 23(c)(i) is carried in addition to sidelights, then such masthead light or all-round light shall be carried at least 1 meter higher than the sidelights.

(e) One of the two or three masthead lights prescribed for a powerdriven vessel when engaged in towing or pushing another vessel shall be placed in the same position as either the forward masthead light or the after masthead light; provided that, if carried on the aftermast, the lowest after masthead light shall be at least 4.5 meters vertically higher than the forward masthead light.

(f) (i) The masthead light or lights prescribed in Rule 23(a) shall be so placed as to be above and clear of all other lights and obstructions except as described in subparagraph (ii).

(ii) When it is impracticable to carry the all-round lights prescribed by Rule 27(b)(i) or Rule 28 below the masthead lights, they may be carried above the after masthead light(s) or vertically in between the forward masthead light(s) and after masthead light(s), provided that in the latter case the requirement of Section 3(c) of this Annex shall be complied with.

(g) The sidelights of a power-driven vessel shall be placed at a height above the hull not greater than three-quarters of that of the forward masthead light. They shall not be so low as to be interfered with by deck lights.

(h) The sidelights, if in a combined lantern and carried on a powerdriven vessel of less than 20 meters in length, shall be placed not less than 1 meter below the masthead light.

(i) When the Rules prescribe two or three lights to be carried in a vertical line, they shall be spaced as follows:

(i) on a vessel of 20 meters in length or more such lights shall be spaced not less than 2 meters apart, and the lowest of these lights shall, except where a towing light is required, be placed at a height of not less than 4 meters above the hull;

(ii) on a vessel of less than 20 meters in length such lights shall be spaced not less than 1 meter apart and the lowest of these lights shall, except where a towing light is required, be placed at a height of not less than 2 meters above the gunwale;

(iii) when three lights are carried they shall be equally spaced.

(j) The lower of the two all-round lights prescribed for a vessel when engaged in fishing shall be at a height above the sidelights not less than twice the distance between the two vertical lights.

(k) The forward anchor light prescribed in Rule 30(a)(i), when two are carried, shall not be less than 4.5 meters above the after one. On a vessel of 50 meters or more in length this forward anchor light shall be placed at a height of not less than 6 meters above the hull.

3. Horizontal positioning and spacing of lights

(a) When two masthead lights are prescribed for a power-driven vessel, the horizontal distance between them shall not be less than one half of the length of the vessel but need not be more than 100 meters. The forward light shall be placed not more than one quarter of the length of the vessel from the stem.

(b) On a power-driven vessel of 20 meters or more in length the sidelights shall not be placed in front of the forward masthead lights. They shall be placed at or near the side of the vessel

(c) When the lights prescribed in Rule 27(b)(i) or Rule 28 are placed vertically between the forward masthead light(s) and the after masthead light(s) these all-round lights shall be placed at a horizontal distance of not less than 2 meters from the fore and aft centerline of the vessel in the athwartship direction.

(d) When only one masthead light is prescribed for a power-driven vessel, this light shall be exhibited forward of amidships; except that a vessel of less then 20 meters in length need not exhibit this light forward of amidships but shall exhibit it as far forward as is practicable.

4. Details of location of direction-indicating lights for fishing vessels, dredgers and vessels engaged in underwater operations

(a) The light indicating the direction of the outlying gear from a vessel engaged in fishing as prescribed in Rule 26(c)(ii) shall be placed at a horizontal distance of not less than 2 meters and not more than 6 meters away from the two all-round red and white lights. This light shall be placed not higher than the all-round white light prescribed in Rule 26(c)(i) and not lower than the sidelights.

(b) The lights and shapes on a vessel engaged in dredging or underwater operations to indicate the obstructed side and/or the side on which it is safe to pass, as prescribed in Rule 27(d)(i) and (ii), shall be placed at the maximum practical horizontal distance, but in no case less than 2 meters, from the lights or shapes prescribed in Rule 27(b)(i) and (ii). In no case shall the upper of these lights or shapes be at a greater height than the lower of the three lights or shapes prescribed in Rule 27(b)(i) and (ii).

5. Screens for sidelights

The sidelights of vessels of 20 meters or more in length shall be fitted with inboard screens painted matt black, and meeting the requirements of Section 9 of this Annex. On vessels of less than 20 meters in length the sidelights, if necessary to meet the requirements of Section 9 of this Annex, shall be fitted with inboard matt black screens. With a combined lantern, using a single vertical filament and a very narrow division between the green and red sections, external screens need not be fitted.

6. Shapes

(a) Shapes shall be black and of the following sizes:

(i) a ball shall have a diameter of not less than 0.6 meter;

(ii) a cone shall have a base diameter of not less than 0.6 meter and a height equal to its diameter;

(iii) a cylinder shall have a diameter of at least 0.6 meter and a height of twice its diameter;

(iv) a diamond shape shall consist of two cones as defined in (ii) above having a common base.

(b) The vertical distance between shapes shall be at least 1.5 meter.

(c) In a vessel of less than 20 meters in length shapes of lesser dimensions but commensurate with the size of the vessel may be used and the distance apart may be correspondingly reduced.

7. Color specification of lights

The chromaticity of all navigation lights shall conform to the following standards, which lie within the boundaries of the area of the diagram specified for each color by the International Commission on Illumination (CIE).

The boundaries of the area for each color are given by indicating the corner coordinates, which are as follows:

(i) White:

x 0.525 0.525 0.452 0.310 0.310 0.443

y 0.382 0.440 0.440 0.348 0.283 0.382

(ii) Green:

x 0.028 0.009 0.300 0.203

y 0.385 0.723 0.511 0.356

(iii) Red:

x 0.680 0.660 0.735 0.721

y 0.320 0.320 0.265 0.259

(iv) Yellow:

x 0.612 0.618 0.575 0.575

y 0.382 0.382 0.425 0.406

8. Intensity of lights

(a) The minimum luminous intensity of lights shall be calculated by using the formula:

$$I = 3.43 \times 10^6 \times T \times D^2 \times K^{-D}$$

where:

I is luminous intensity in candelas under service conditions,

T is threshold factor 2×10^{-7} lux,

D is range of visibility (luminous range) of the light in nautical miles,

K is atmospheric transmissivity. For prescribed lights the value of K shall be 0.8, corresponding to a meteorological visibility of approximately 13 nautical miles.

(b) A selection of figures derived from the formula is given in the following table:

Range of visibility (luminous range) of light in nautica luminous miles	Luminous lintensity of light in candelas for K = 0.8
D	I
1	0.9
2	4.3
3	12
4	27
5	52
6	94

Note: The maximum luminous intensity of navigation lights should be limited to avoid undue glare. This shall not be achieved by a variable control of the luminous intensity.

9. Horizontal sectors

(a)

(i) In the forward direction, sidelights as fitted on the vessel shall show the minimum required intensities. The intensities shall decrease to reach practical cut-off between 1 degree and 3 degrees outside the prescribed sectors.

(ii) For sternlights and masthead lights and at 22.5 degrees abaft the beam for sidelights, the minimum required intensities shall be maintained over the arc of the horizon up to 5 degrees within the limits of the sectors prescribed in Rule 21. From 5 degrees within the prescribed sectors the intensity may decrease by 50 percent up to the prescribed limits; it shall decrease steadily to reach practical cut-off at not more than 5 degrees outside the prescribed sectors.

(b)

(i) All-round lights shall be so located as not to be obscured by masts, topmasts or structures within angular sectors of more than 6 degrees, except anchor lights prescribed in Rule 30, which need not be placed at an impracticable height above the hull.

(ii) If it is impracticable to comply with paragraph (b)(i) of this section by exhibiting only one all-round light, two all-round lights shall be used suitably positioned or screened so that they appear, as far as practicable, as one light at a distance of one mile."

10. Vertical sectors

(a) The vertical sectors of electric lights as fitted, with the exception of lights on sailing vessels underway shall ensure that:

(i) at least the required minimum intensity is maintained at all angles from 5 degrees above to 5 degrees below the horizontal;

(ii) at least 60 percent of the required minimum intensity is maintained from 7.5 degrees above to 7.5 degrees below the horizontal.

(b) In the case of sailing vessels underway the vertical sectors of electric lights as fitted shall ensure that:

(i) at least the required minimum intensity is maintained at all angles from 5 degrees above to 5 degrees below the horizontal;
(ii) at least 50 percent of the required minimum intensity is maintained from 25 degrees above to 25 degrees below the horizontal.
(c) In the case of lights other than electric these specifications shall be met as closely as possible.

11. Intensity of non-electric lights

Non-electric lights shall so far as practicable comply with the minimum intensities, as specified in the Table given in Section 8 of this Annex.

12. Maneuvering light

Notwithstanding the provisions of paragraph 2(f) of this Annex the maneuvering light described in Rule 34(b) shall be placed in the same fore and aft vertical plane as the masthead light or lights and, where practicable, at a minimum height of 2 meters vertically above the forward masthead light, provided that it shall be carried not less than 2 meters vertically above or below the after masthead light. On a vessel where only one masthead light is carried the maneuvering light, if fitted, shall be carried where it can best be seen, not less than 2 meters vertically apart from the masthead light.

13. High Speed Craft⋆

(a) The masthead light of high speed craft may be placed at a height related to the breadth of the craft lower than that prescribed in paragraph 2(a)(i) of this Annex, provided that the base angle of the isosceles triangles formed by the sidelights and masthead light, when seen in end elevation, is not less than 27°.
(b) On high-speed craft of 50 meters or more in length, the vertical separation between foremast and mainmast light of 4.5 meters required by paragraph 2 (a)(ii) of this annex may be modified provided that such distance shall not be less than the value determined by the following formula:

$$y = (a +17Y)C/1000 \qquad +2$$

where: y is the height of the masthead light above the foremast light in metres;
      a   is the height of the foremast light above the water service in service condition in metres;
      Y   is the trim in service condition in degrees;
      C   is the horizontal separation of masthead lights in metres. (as of 11/29/03 **INTL**)
⋆ Refer to the International Code of Safety for High-Speed Craft, 1944 and to the International Code of Safety for High-Speed Craft, 2000.

14. Approval

The construction of lights and shapes and the installation of lights on board the vessel shall be to the satisfaction of the appropriate authority of the State whose flag the vessel is entitled to fly.

33 CFR 85: ANNEX II - INLAND ADDITIONAL SIGNALS FOR FISHING VESSELS

§85.1. General
The lights mentioned herein shall, if exhibited in pursuance of Rule 26(d), be placed where they can best be seen. They shall be at least 0.9 meter apart but at a lower level than lights prescribed in Rule 26(b)(i) and (c)(i) contained in the Inland Navigational Rules Act of 1980. The lights shall be visible all around the horizon at a distance of at least 1 mile but at a lesser distance from the lights prescribed by these Rules for fishing vessels.

§ 85.3 Signals for trawlers
(a) Vessels when engaged in trawling, whether using demersal or pelagic gear, may exhibit:

(1) When shooting their nets: two white lights in a vertical line;

(2) When hauling their nets: one white light over one red light in a vertical line;

(3) When the net has come fast upon an obstruction: two red lights in a vertical line.

(b) Each vessel engaged in pair trawling may exhibit:

(1) By night, a searchlight directed forward and in the direction of the other vessel of the pair;

(2) When shooting or hauling their nets or when their nets have come fast upon an obstruction, the lights prescribed in paragraph (a) of this section.

§ 85.5 Signals for purse seiners
Vessels engaged in fishing with purse seine gear may exhibit two yellow lights in a vertical line. These lights shall flash alternately every second and with equal light and occultation duration. These lights may be exhibited only when the vessel is hampered by its fishing gear

ANNEX II: INTERNATIONAL ADDITIONAL SIGNALS FOR FISHING VESSELS

1. General
The lights mentioned herein shall, if exhibited in pursuance of Rule 26(d), be placed where they can best be seen. They shall be at least 0.9 meter apart but at a lower level than lights prescribed in Rule 26(b)(i) and (c)(i). The lights shall be visible all around the horizon at a distance of at least 1 mile but at a lesser distance than the lights prescribed by these Rules for fishing vessels.

2. Signals for trawlers
(a) Vessels of 20 meters or more in length when engaged in trawling, whether

using demersal or pelagic gear, shall exhibit:

(i) when shooting their nets: two white lights in a vertical line;

(ii) when hauling their nets: one white light over one red light in a vertical line;

(iii) when the net has come fast upon an obstruction: two red lights in a vertical line.

(b) Each vessel of 20 meters or more in length engaged in pair trawling shall exhibit:

(i) by night, a searchlight directed forward and in the direction of the other vessel of the pair;

(ii) when shooting or hauling their nets or when their nets have come fast upon an obstruction, the lights prescribed in 2(a) above.

(c) A vessel of less than 20 meters in length engaged in trawling, whether using demersal or pelagic gear, or engaged in pair trawling, may exhibit the lights prescribed in paragraphs (a) or (b) of this section, as appropriate.

3. Signals for purse seiners

Vessels engaged in fishing with purse seine gear may exhibit two yellow lights in a vertical line. These lights shall flash alternately every second and with equal light and occultation duration. These lights may be exhibited only when the vessel is hampered by its fishing gear.

33 CFR 86: ANNEX III - INLAND TECHNICAL DETAILS OF SOUND SIGNAL APPLIANCES

SUBPART A – WHISTLES

§ 86.01 Frequencies and range of audibility

The fundamental frequency of the signal shall lie within the range 70-525 Hz The range of audibility of the signal from a whistle shall be determined by those frequencies, which may include the fundamental and/or one or more higher frequencies, which lie within the frequency ranges and provide the sound pressure levels specified in §86.05.

§ 86.03 Limits of fundamental frequencies

To ensure a wide variety of whistle characteristics, the fundamental frequency of a whistle shall be between the following limits:

(a) 70-200 Hz, for a vessel 200 meters or more in length;

(b) 130-350 Hz, for a vessel 75 meters but less than 200 meters in length;

(c) 250-525 Hz, for a vessel less than 75 meters in length.

§ 86.05 Sound signal intensity and range of audibility

A whistle on a vessel shall provide, in the direction of the forward axis of the whistle and at a distance of 1 meter from it, a sound pressure level in at least one

Length of Vessel in Meters	Fundamental Frequency Range (Hz)	For Measured Frequencies (Hz)	1/3-octave band level at 1 meter in dB referred to 2x10-5 N/M2	Audibility range in Nautical Miles
200 or more	70-200	130-180	145	2.0
		180-250	143	
		250-1200	140	
75 but less than 200	130-350	130-180	140	1.5
		180-250	138	
		250-1200	134	
20 but less than 75	250-525	250-450	130	1.0
		450-800	125	
		800-1600	121	
12 but less than 20	250-525	250-450	120	0.5
		450-800	115	
		800-2100	111	

1/3-octave band of not less than the appropriate figure given in Table 86.05 within the following frequency ranges (± 1 percent):
(a) 130-1200 Hz, for a vessel 75 meters or more in length;
(b) 250-1600 Hz, for a vessel 20 meters but less than 75 meters in length;
(c) 250-2100 Hz, for a vessel 12 meters but less than 20 meters in length.

NOTE: The range of audibility in the table above is for information and is approximately the range at which a whistle may usually be heard on its forward axis in conditions of still air on board a vessel having average background noise level at the listening posts (taken to be 68 dB in the octave band centered on 250 Hz and 63 dB in the octave band centered on 500 Hz). In practice the range at which a whistle may be heard is extremely variable and depends critically on weather conditions; the values given can be regarded as typical but under conditions of strong wind or high ambient noise level at the listening post the range may be much reduced.

§ 86.07 Directional properties
The sound pressure level of a directional whistle shall be not more than 4 dB below the sound pressure level specified in § 86.05 in any direction in the horizontal plane within + 45 degrees of the forward axis. The sound pressure level of the whistle in any other direction in the horizontal plane shall not be more than 10 dB less than the sound pressure level specified for the forward axis, so that the range of audibility in any direction will be at least half the range required on the forward axis. The sound pressure level shall be measured in that one-third octave band which determines the audibility range.

§ 86.09 Positioning of whistles

(a) When a directional whistle is to be used as the only whistle on the vessel and is permanently installed, it shall be installed with its forward axis directed forward.

(b) A whistle shall be placed as high as practicable on a vessel, in order to reduce interception of the emitted sound by obstructions and also to minimize hearing damage risk to personnel. The sound pressure level of the vessel's own signal at listening posts shall not exceed 110 dB(A) and so far as practicable should not exceed 100 dB(A).

§ 86.11 Fitting of more than one whistle

If whistles are fitted at a distance apart of more than 100 meters, they shall not be sounded simultaneously.

§ 86.13 Combined whistle systems

(a) A combined whistle system is a number of whistles (sound emitting sources) operated together. For the purposes of the Rules a combined whistle system is to be regarded as a single whistle.

(b) The whistles of a combined system shall: (1) Be located at a distance apart of not more than 100 meters, (2) Be sounded simultaneously, (3) Each have a fundamental frequency different from those of the others by at least 10 Hz, and (4) Have a tonal characteristic appropriate for the length of vessel which shall be evidenced by at least two-thirds of the whistles in the combined system having fundamental frequencies falling within the limits prescribed in § 86.03, or if there are only two whistles in the combined system, by the higher fundamental frequency falling within the limits prescribed § 86.03.

NOTE: If due to the presence of obstructions the sound field of a single whistle or of one of the whistles referred to in §86.11 is likely to have a zone of greatly reduced signal level a combined whistle system should be fitted so as to overcome this reduction.

§ 86.15 Towing vessel whistles

A power-driven vessel normally engaged in pushing ahead or towing alongside may, at all times, use a whistle whose characteristic falls within the limits prescribed by § 86.03 for the longest customary composite length of the vessel and its tow.

Subpart B - Bell or gong
§ 86.21 Intensity of signal

A bell or gong, or other device having similar sound characteristics shall produce a sound pressure level of not less than 110 dB at 1 meter.

§ 86.23 Construction

Bells and gongs shall be made of corrosion-resistant material and designed to give a clear tone. The diameter of the mouth of the bell shall be not less than 300 mm for vessels of more than 20 meters in length, and shall be not less than 200 mm for vessels of 12 to 20 meters in length. The mass of the striker shall be not less than 3 percent of the mass of the bell. The striker shall be capable of manual operation.

NOTE: When practicable, a power-driven bell striker is recommended to ensure constant force.

Subpart C - Approval
§ 86.31 Approval [Reserved]

ANNEX III: INTERNATIONAL TECHNICAL DETAILS OF SOUND SIGNAL APPLIANCES

1. Whistles
(a) Frequencies and range of audibility
The fundamental frequency of the signal shall lie within the range 70-700 Hz. The range of audibility of the signal from a whistle shall be determined by those frequencies, which may include the fundamental and/or one or more higher frequencies, which lie within the range 180-700 Hz (+/- 1 percent) for a vessel of 20 meters or more in length or 180-2100 Hz (+/- 1 percent) for a vessel of less than 20 meters in length (as of 11/19/03) and which provide the sound pressure levels specified in paragraph 1(c) below.
(b) Limits of fundamental frequencies
To ensure a wide variety of whistle characteristics, the fundamental frequency of a whistle shall be between the following limits:
(i) 70-200 Hz, for a vessel 200 meters or more in length;
(ii) 130-350 Hz, for a vessel 75 meters but less than 200 meters in length;
(iii) 250-700 Hz, for a vessel less than 75 meters in length.
(c) Sound signal intensity and range of audibility
A whistle fitted in a vessel shall provide, in the direction of maximum intensity of the whistle and at a distance of 1 meter from it, a sound pressure level in at least one 1/3-octave band within the range of frequencies 180-700 Hz (+/- 1 percent) for a vessel of 20 meters or more in length, or 180-2100Hz (+/- 1 percent) for a vessel less than 20 meters in length (as of 11/29/03), of not less than the appropriate figure given in the table below.

Length of Vessel in Meters	1/3 Octave band level at 1 meter in dB referred to 2×10^{-5} N/M^2	Audibility range in Nautical Miles
200 or more	143	2.0

75 but less than 200	138	1.5
20 but less than 75	130	1.0
Less than 20	120*/115** /111***	0.5

* When the measured frequencies lie within the range 180-450Hz
**When the measured frequencies lie within the range 450-800Hz
*** When the measured frequencies lie within the range 800-2100Hz (as of 11/29/03)

NOTE: The range of audibility in the table above is for information and is approximately the range at which a whistle may be heard on its forward axis with 90 percent probability in conditions of still air on board a vessel having average background noise level at the listening posts (taken to be 68 dB in the octave band centered on 250 Hz and 63 dB in the octave band centered on 500 Hz). In practice the range at which a whistle may be heard is extremely variable and depends critically on weather conditions; the values given can be regarded as typical but under conditions of strong wind or high ambient noise level at the listening post the range may be much reduced.

(d) Directional properties
The sound pressure level of a directional whistle shall be not more than 4 dB below the prescribed sound pressure level on the axis at any direction in the horizontal plane within ± 45 degrees of the axis. The sound pressure level at any other direction in the horizontal plane shall be not more than 10 dB below the prescribed sound pressure level on the axis, so that the range in any direction will be at least half the range on the forward axis. The sound pressure level shall be measured in that one-third octave band which determines the audibility range.
(e) Positioning of whistles
When a directional whistle is to be used as the only whistle on a vessel, it shall be installed with its maximum intensity directed straight ahead.
A whistle shall be placed as high as practicable on a vessel, in order to reduce interception of the emitted sound by obstructions and also to minimize hearing damage risk to personnel. The sound pressure level of the vessel's own signal at listening posts shall not exceed 110 dB(A) and so far as practicable should not exceed 100 dB(A).
(f) Fitting of more than one whistle
If whistles are fitted at a distance apart of more than 100 meters, it shall be so arranged that they are not sounded simultaneously.
(g) Combined whistle systems
If due to the presence of obstructions the sound field of a single whistle or of one of the whistles referred to in paragraph 1(f) above is likely to have a zone of greatly reduced signal level, it is recommended that a combined whistle system be fit-

ted so as to overcome this reduction. For the purposes of the Rules a combined whistle system is to be regarded as a single whistle. The whistles of a combined system shall be located at a distance apart of not more than 100 meters and arranged to be sounded simultaneously. The frequency of any one whistle shall differ from those of the others by at least 10 Hz.

2. Bell or gong
(a) Intensity of signal
A bell or gong, or other device having similar sound characteristics shall produce a sound pressure level of not less than 110 dB at a distance of 1 meter from it.
(b) Construction
Bells and gongs shall be made of corrosion-resistant material and designed to give a clear tone. The diameter of the mouth of the bell shall be not less than 300 mm for vessels of 20 meters or more in length. (Bell specifications aboard vessels 20 meters and less deleted as of 11/29/03.) Where practicable, a power-driven bell striker is recommended to ensure constant force but manual operation shall be possible. The mass of the striker shall be not less than 3 percent of the mass of the bell.

3. Approval
The construction of sound signal appliances, their performance and their installation on board the vessel shall be to the satisfaction of the appropriate authority of the State whose flag the vessel is entitled to fly.

33 CFR 87: ANNEX IV – INLAND DISTRESS SIGNALS

§ 87.1 Need of assistance
The following signals, used or exhibited either together or separately, indicate distress and need of assistance:
(a) A gun or other explosive signal fired at intervals of about a minute;
(b) A continuous sounding with any fog-signaling apparatus;
(c) Rockets or shells, throwing red stars fired one at a time at short intervals;
(d) A signal made by radiotelegraphy or by any other signaling method consisting of the group . . .– – –. . . (SOS) in the Morse Code;
(e) A signal sent by radiotelephony consisting of the spoken word "Mayday";
(f) The International Code Signal of distress indicated by N.C.;
(g) A signal consisting of a square flag having above or below it a ball or anything resembling a ball;
(h) Flames on the vessel (as from a burning tar barrel, oil barrel, etc.);
(I) A rocket parachute flare or a hand flare showing a red light;
(j) A smoke signal giving off orange-colored smoke;
(k) Slowly and repeatedly raising and lowering arms outstretched to each side;
(I) The radiotelegraph alarm signal;

(m) The radiotelephone alarm signal;

(n) Signals transmitted by emergency position-indicating radio beacons;

(o) Signals transmitted by radio communication systems, including survival craft radar transponders meeting the requirements of 47 CFR 80.1095.

(p) A high intensity white light flashing at regular intervals from 50 to 70 times per minute.

§ 87.3 Exclusive use

The use or exhibition of any of the foregoing signals except for the purpose of indicating distress and need of assistance and the use of other signals which may be confused with any of the above signals is prohibited.

§ 87.5 Supplemental signals

Attention is drawn to the relevant sections of the International Code of Signals, the Merchant Ship Search and Rescue Manual, the International Telecommunication Union Radio Regulations, and the following signals:

(a) A piece of orange-colored canvas with either a black square and circle or other appropriate symbol (for identification from the air);

(b) A dye marker.

ANNEX IV: INTERNATIONAL DISTRESS SIGNALS

1. The following signals, used or exhibited either together or separately, indicate distress and need of assistance:

(a) a gun or other explosive signal fired at intervals of about a minute;

(b) a continuous sounding with any fog-signaling apparatus;

(c) rockets or shells, throwing red stars fired one at a time at short intervals;

(d) a signal made by radiotelegraphy or by any other signaling method consisting of the group . . .- - -. . . (SOS) in the Morse Code;

(e) a signal sent by radiotelephony consisting of the spoken word "Mayday";

(f) the International Code Signal of distress indicated by N.C.;

(g) a signal consisting of a square flag having above or below it a ball or anything resembling a ball;

(h) flames on the vessel (as from a burning tar barrel, oil barrel, etc.);

(i) a rocket parachute flare or a hand flare showing a red light;

(j) a smoke signal giving off orange-colored smoke;

(k) slowly and repeatedly raising and lowering arms outstretched to each side;

(I) the radiotelegraph alarm signal;

(m) the radiotelephone alarm signal;

(n) signals transmitted by emergency position-indicating radio beacons;

(o) approved signals transmitted by radio communication systems, including survival craft radar transponders.

2. The use or exhibition of any of the foregoing signals except for the purpose of

indicating distress and need of assistance and the use of other signals which may be confused with any of the above signals is prohibited.

3. Attention is drawn to the relevant sections of the International Code of Signals, the Merchant Ship Search and Rescue Manual and the following signals:

(a) a piece of orange-colored canvas with either a black square and circle or other appropriate symbol (for identification from the air);

(b) a dye marker.

33 CFR 88: ANNEX V - PILOT RULES

§ 88.01 Purpose and applicability
This Part applies to all vessels operating on United States inland waters and to United States vessels operating on the Canadian waters of the Great Lakes to the extent there is no conflict with Canadian law.

§ 88.03 Definitions
The terms used in this part have the same meaning as defined in the Inland Navigational Rules Act of 1980.

§ 88.05 Copy of Rules
After January 1, 1983, the operator of each self-propelled vessel 12 meters or more in length shall carry on board and maintain for ready reference a copy of the Inland Navigation Rules.

§ 88.09 Temporary exemption from light and shape requirements when operating under bridges
A vessel's navigation lights and shapes may be lowered if necessary to pass under a bridge.

§ 88.11 Law enforcement vessels
(a) Law enforcement vessels may display a flashing blue light when engaged in direct law enforcement or public safety activities. This light must be located so that it does not interfere with the visibility of the vessel's navigation lights.

(b) The blue light described in this section may be displayed by law enforcement vessels of the United States and the States and their political subdivisions.

§ 88.12 Public Safety Activities
(a) Vessels engaged in government sanctioned public safety activities, and commercial vessels performing similar functions, may display an alternately flashing red and yellow light signal. This identification light signal must be located so that it does not interfere with the visibility of the vessel's navigation lights. The identification light signal may be used only as an identification signal and conveys no

special privilege. Vessels using the identification light signal during public safety activities must abide by the Inland Navigation Rules, and must not presume that the light or the exigency gives them precedence or right of way.

(b) Public safety activities include but are not limited to patrolling marine parades, regattas, or special water celebrations; traffic control; salvage; firefighting; medical assistance; assisting disabled vessels; and search and rescue.

§ 88.13 Lights on moored barges

(a) The following barges shall display at night and if practicable in periods of restricted visibility the lights described in paragraph (b) of this section:

(1) Every barge projecting into a buoyed or restricted channel. (2) Every barge so moored that it reduces the available navigable width of any channel to less than 80 meters.

(3) Barges moored in groups more than two barges wide or to a maximum width of over 25 meters.

(4) Every barge not moored parallel to the bank or dock.

(b) Barges described in paragraph (a) of this section shall carry two unobstructed all-round white lights of an intensity to be visible for at least one nautical mile and meeting the technical requirements as prescribed in § 84.15 of this chapter.

(c) A barge or a group of barges at anchor or made fast to one or more mooring buoys or other similar device, in lieu of the provisions of Inland Navigation Rule 30, may carry unobstructed all-round white lights of an intensity to be visible for at least one nautical mile that meet the requirements of § 84.15 of this chapter and shall be arranged as follows:

(1) Any barge that projects from a group formation, shall be lighted on its outboard corners.

(2) On a single barge moored in water where other vessels normally navigate on both sides of the barge, lights shall be placed to mark the corner extremities of the barge.

(3) On barges moored in group formation, moored in water where other vessels normally navigate on both sides of the group, lights shall be placed to mark the corner extremities of the group. (d) The following are exempt from the requirements of this section:

(1) A barge or group of barges moored in a slip or slough used primarily for mooring purposes.

(2) A barge or group of barges moored behind a pierhead. (3) A barge less than 20 meters in length when moored in a special anchorage area designated in accordance with § 109.10 of this chapter.

(e) Barges moored in well-illuminated areas are exempt from the lighting requirements of this section. These areas are as follows:

CHICAGO SANITARY SHIP CANAL
(1) Mile 293.2 to 293.9
(3) Mile 295.2 to 296.1
(5) Mile 297.5 to 297.8

(7) Mile 298 to 298.2
(9) Mile 298.6 to 298.8
(11) Mile 299.3 to 299.4
(13) Mile 299.8 to 300.5
(15) Mile 303 to 303.2
(17) Mile 303.7 to 303.9
(19) Mile 305.7 to 305.8
(21) Mile 310.7 to 310.9
(23) Mile 311 to 311.2
(25) Mile 312.5 to 312.6
(27) Mile 313.8 to 314.2
(29) Mile 314.6
(31) Mile 314.8 to 315.3
(33) Mile 315.7 to 316
(35) Mile 316.8
(37) Mile 316.85 to 317.05
(39) Mile 317.5
(41) Mile 318.4 to 318.9
(43) Mile 318.7 to 318.8
(45) Mile 320 to 320.3

Calumet Sag Channel
(61) Mile 316.5

Little Calumet River
(71) Mile 321.2
(73) Mile 322.3

Calumet River
(81) Mile 328.5 to 328.7
(83) Mile 329.2 to 329.4
(85) Mile 330 west bank to 330.2
(87) Mile 331.4 to 331.6
(89) Mile 332.2 to 332.4
(91) Mile 332.6 to 332.8

Cumberland River
(101) Mile 126.8
(103) Mile 191

§ 88.15 Lights on dredge pipelines
Dredge pipelines that are floating or supported on trestles shall display the following lights at night and in periods of restricted visibility. (a) One row of yellow lights. The lights must be:

(1) Flashing 50 to 70 times per minute,

(2) Visible all around the horizon,

(3) Visible for at least 2 miles on a clear dark night,

(4) Not less than 1 and not more than 3.5 meters above the water,

(5) Approximately equally spaced, and

(6) Not more than 10 meters apart where the pipeline crosses a navigable channel. Where the pipeline does not cross a navigable channel the lights must be sufficient in number to clearly show the pipeline's length and course.

(b) Two red lights at each end of the pipeline, including the ends in a channel
where the pipeline is separated to allow vessels to pass (whether open or closed).
The lights must be:

(1) Visible all around the horizon, and

(2) Visible for at least 2 miles on a clear dark night, and

(3) One meter apart in a vertical line with the lower light at the same height
above the water as the flashing yellow light.

—INLAND—
INTERPRETATIVE RULES
33 CFR 90

§ 90.1 Purpose
This part contains the interpretative rules for the Inland Rules.
These interpretative rules are intended as a guide to assist the public
and promote compliance with the Inland Rules.

§ 90.3 Pushing vessel and vessel being pushed: Composite unit
Rule 24(b) of the Inland Rules states that when a pushing vessel
and a vessel being pushed ahead are rigidly connected in a composite
unit, they are regarded as a power-driven vessel and must
exhibit the lights prescribed in Rule 23. A "composite unit" is interpreted
to be the combination of a pushing vessel and a vessel being
pushed ahead that are rigidly connected by mechanical means so
they react to sea and swell as one vessel. Mechanical means does
not include lines, wires, hawsers, or chains.

§ 90.5 Lights for moored vessels
A vessel at anchor includes a vessel made fast to one or more
mooring buoys or other similar device attached to the ocean floor.
Such vessels may be lighted as a vessel at anchor in accordance
with Rule 30, or may be lighted on the corners in accordance with 33
CFR 88.13.

§ 90.7 Sidelights for unmanned barges

An unmanned barge being towed may use the exception of COLREGS Rule 24(h). However, this exception only applies to the vertical sector requirements.

—INTERNATIONAL—
INTERPRETATIVE RULES
33 CFR 82

§ 82.1 Purpose

This part contains the interpretative rules concerning the 72 COLREGS that are adopted by the Coast Guard for the guidance of the public.

§ 82.3 Pushing vessel and vessel being pushed: Composite unit

Rule 24(b) of the 72 COLREGS states that when a pushing vessel and a vessel being pushed ahead are rigidly connected in a composite unit, they are regarded as a power-driven vessel and must exhibit the lights under Rule 23. A "composite unit" is interpreted to be a pushing vessel that is rigidly connected by mechanical means to a vessel being pushed so they react to sea and swell as one vessel. "Mechanical means" does not include the following:
(a) Lines.
(b) Hawsers.
(c) Wires.
(d) Chains.

§ 82.5 Lights for moored vessels

For the purposes of Rule 30 of the 72 COLREGS, a vessel at anchor includes a barge made fast to one or more mooring buoys or other similar device attached to the sea or river floor. Such a barge may be lighted as a vessel at anchor in accordance with Rule 30, or may be lighted on the corners in accordance with 33 CFR 88.13.

§ 82.7 Sidelights for unmanned barges

An unmanned barge being towed may use the exception of COLREGS Rule 24(h). However, this exception only applies to the vertical sector requirements.

COLREGS DEMARCATION LINES 33 CFR 80 GENERAL

80.01 General basis and purpose of demarcation lines.

The regulations in this part establish the lines of demarcation (printed on the nautical charts in magenta), delineating those waters upon which mariners shall comply with the International Regulations for Preventing Collisions at Sea, 1972 (72 COLREGS) and those waters upon which mariners shall comply with the Inland Navigation Rules. The waters inside of the lines are Inland Rules waters. The waters outside the lines are COLREGS waters. This notice is divided into two parts The first is a catalog listing the six general locations where COLREGS exist (Atlantic Coast, Gulf Coast, Pacific Coast, etc.). Also shown are the Coast Guard Districts concerned within the listed locations. Finally, in the first section are the specific section citations where you can find the COLREGS boundaries.

In the second part of this notice you'll find each citation (such as §80.125) outlining the actual position of the demarcation lines separating International from Inland Rules. —The Editors

ATLANTIC COAST

FIRST DISTRICT

80.105 Calais, ME to
Cape Small, ME.
80.110 Casco Bay, ME.
80.115 Portland Head, ME to
Cape Ann, MA.
80.120 Cape Ann, MA to
Marblehead Neck, MA.
80.125 Marblehead Neck, MA to
Nahant, MA.
80.130 Boston Harbor entrance.
80.135 Hull, MA to
Race Point, MA.
80.145 Race Point, MA to
Watch Hill, Rl.
80.150 Block Island, Rl.
80.155 Watch Hill, Rl to
Montauk Point, NY.
80.160 Montauk Point, NY
to Atlantic Beach, NY.
80.165 New York Harbor.
80.170 Sandy Hook, NJ to
Tom's River, NJ.

FIFTH DISTRICT

80.501 Tom's River, N.J. to
Cape May, NJ.
80.503 Delaware Bay.
80.505 Cape Henlopen, DE to
Cape Charles, VA.
80.510 Chesapeake Bay
Entrance, VA.
80.515 Cape Henry, VA to
Cape Hatteras, NC
80.520 Cape Hatteras, NC to
Cape Lookout, NC.
80.525 Cape Lookout, NC to
Cape Fear, NC.
80.530 Cape Fear, NC to New
River Inlet, NC.

SEVENTH DISTRICT

80.703 Little River Inlet, SC to
Cape Romain, SC.
80.707 Cape Romain, SC to
Sullivans Island, SC.
80.710 Charleston Harbor, SC.
80.712 Morris Island, SC to

Hilton Head Island, SC.
80.715 Savannah River.
80.717 Tybee Island, GA to
St. Simons Island, GA.
80.720 St. Simons Island, GA to
Amelia Island, FL.
80.723 Amelia Island, FL to
Cape Canaveral, FL.
80.727 Cape Canaveral, FL to
Miami Beach, FL.
80.730 Miami Harbor, FL.
80.735 Miami, FL to
Long Key, FL.

Perdido Bay, FL.
80.815 Mobile Bay, AL to
the Chandeleur Island, LA.
80.825 Mississippi Passes, LA.
80.830 Mississippi Passes, LA to
Point Au Fer, LA.
80.835 Point Au Fer, LA to
Calcasieu Pass, LA.
80.840 Sabine Pass, TX to
Galveston, TX.
80.845 Galveston, TX to
Freeport, TX.
80.850 Brazos River, TX to
the Rio Grande, TX.

PUERTO RICO AND VIRGIN ISLANDS
SEVENTH DISTRICT
80.738 Puerto Rico and
Virgin Islands

GULF COAST
SEVENTH DISTRICT
80.740 Long Key, FL to
Cape Sable, FL.
80.745 Cape Sable, FL to
Cape Romano, FL.
80.748 Cape Romano, FL to
Sanibel Island, FL.
80.750 Sanibel Island, FL to
St. Petersburg, FL.
80.753 St. Petersburg, FL to
Anclote, FL.
80.755 Anclote, FL to
the Suncoast Keys, FL.
80.757 Suncoast Keys, FL to
Horseshoe Point, FL.
80.760 Horseshoe Point, FL to
Rock Island, FL.

EIGHTH DISTRICT
80.805 Rock Island, FL to Cape
San Blas, FL.
80.810 Cape San Blas, FL to

PACIFIC COAST
ELEVENTH DISTRICT
80.1102 Santa Catalina Island,
CA.
80.1104 San Diego Harbor, CA.
80.1106 Mission Bay, CA.
80.1108 Oceanside Harbor, CA.
80.1110 Dana Point Harbor, CA.
80.1112 Newport Bay, CA.
80.1114 San Pedro Bay-
Anaheim Bay, CA.
80.1116 Redondo Harbor, CA.
80.1118 Marina Del Rey, CA.
80.1120 Port Hueneme, CA.
80.1122 Channel Islands
Harbor, CA.
80.1124 Ventura Marina, CA.
80.1126 Santa Barbara Harbor,
CA.
80.1130 San Luis Obispo
Bay, CA.
80.1132 Estero-Morro Bay, CA.
80.1134 Monterey Harbor, CA.
80.1136 Moss Landing Harbor,
CA.
80.1138 Santa Cruz Harbor, CA.
80.1140 Pillar Point Harbor, CA.

80.1142 San Francisco Harbor, CA.
80.1144 Bodega and Tomales Bay, CA.
80.1146 Albion River, CA.
80.1148 Noyo River, CA.
80.1150 Arcato-Humboldt Bay, CA.
80.1152 Crescent City Harbor, CA.

THIRTEENTH DISTRICT
80.1305 Chetco River, OR.
80.1310 Rogue River, OR.
80.1315 Coquille River, OR.
80.1320 Coos Bay, OR.
80.1325 Umpqua River, OR.
80.1330 Siuslaw River, OR.
80.1335 Alsea Bay, OR.
80.1340 Yaquina Bay, OR.
80.1345 Depoe Bay, OR.
80.1350 Netarts Bay, OR.
80.1355 Tillamook Bay, OR.
80.1360 Nehalem River, OR.
80.1365 Columbia River Entrance, OR/WA.
80.1370 Willapa Bay, WA.
80.1375 Grays Harbor, WA.
80.1380 Quillayute River, WA.
80.1385 Strait of Juan de Fuca.
80.1390 Haro Strait and Strait of Georgia.
80.1395 Puget Sound and adjacent waters.

PACIFIC ISLANDS
FOURTEENTH DISTRICT
80.1410 Hawaiian Island Exemption from General Rule.
80.1420 Mamala Bay, Oahu, Hl.
80.1430 Kaneohe Bay, Oahu, Hl.
80.1440 Port Allen, Kauai, HI.
80.1450 Nawiliwili Harbor, Kauai, Hl.

80.1460 Kahului Harbor, Maui, Hl.
80.1470 Kawaihae Harbor, Hawaii, Hl.
80.1480 Hilo Harbor, Hawaii, Hl.
80.1490 Apra Harbor, U.S. Territory of Guam.
80.1495 U.S. Pacific Island Possessions.

ALASKA
SEVENTEENTH DISTRICT
80.1705 Alaska.

GENERAL
§ 80.01 General basis and purpose of demarcation lines.
(a) The regulations in this part establish the lines of demarcation delineating those waters upon which mariners shall comply with the International Regulations for Preventing Collisions at Sea, 1972 (72 COLREGS) and those waters upon which mariners shall comply with the Inland Navigation Rules.
(b) The waters inside of the lines are Inland Rules Waters. The waters outside the lines are COLREGS Waters.

ATLANTIC COAST
FIRST DISTRICT
§ 80.105 Calais, ME to Cape Small, ME.
The 72 COLREGS shall apply on the harbors, bays, and inlets on the east coast of Maine from International Bridge at Calais, ME to the southwesternmost extremity of Bald Head at Cape Small.
§ 80.110 Casco Bay, ME.
(a) A line drawn from the southwesternmost extremity of

Bald Head at Cape Small to the southeasternmost extremity of Ragged Island; thence to the southern tangent of Jaquish Island thence to Little Mark Island Monument Light; thence to the northernmost extremity of Jewell Island.

(b) A line drawn from the tower on Jewell Island charted in approximate position latitude 43° 40.6' N. longitude 70° 05.9'W. to the northeasternmost extremity of Outer Green Island.

(c) A line drawn from the southwesternmost extremity of Outer Green Island to Ram Island Ledge Light; thence to Portland Head Light.

§ 80.115 Portland Head, ME to Cape Ann, MA.

(a) Except inside lines specifically described in this section, the 72 COLREGS shall apply on the harbors, bays, and inlets on the east coast of Maine, New Hampshire, and Massachusetts from Portland Head to Halibut Point at Cape Ann.

(b) A line drawn from the southernmost tower on Gerrish Island charted in approximate position latitude 43°04.0' N. longitude 70°41.2'W. to Whale-back Light; thence to Jeffrey Point Light 2A; thence to the northeasternmost extremity of Frost Point.

(c) A line drawn from the northernmost extremity of Farm Point to Annisquam Harbor Light.

§ 80.120 Cape Ann, MA to Marblehead Neck, MA.

(a) Except inside lines specifically described in this section, the 72 COLREGS shall apply on the harbors, bays and inlets on the east coast of Massachusetts from Halibut Point at Cape Ann to Marblehead Neck.

(b) A line drawn from Gloucester Harbor Breakwater Light to the twin towers charted in approximate position latitude 42°35.1' N. longitude 70°41.6'W.

(c) A line drawn from the westernmost extremity of Gales Point to the easternmost extremity of House Island; thence to Bakers Island Light; thence to Marblehead Light.

§ 80.125 Marblehead Neck, MA to Nahant, MA.

The 72 COLREGS apply on the harbors, bays, and inlets on the east coast of Massachusetts from Marblehead Neck to the easternmost tower at Nahant, charted in approximate position latitude 42°25.4' N., longitude 70°54.6'W.

§ 80.130 Boston Harbor entrance.

A line drawn from the easternmost tower at Nahant, charted in approximate position latitude 42° 25.4' N., longitude 70°54.6'W., to Boston Lighted Horn Buoy "B"; thence to the easternmost radio tower at Hull, charted in approximate position latitude 42°16.7' N., longitude 70°52.6'W.

§ 80.135 Hull, MA to Race Point, MA.

(a) Except inside lines described in this section, the 72 COLREGS apply on the harbors, bays, and inlets on the east coast of Massachusetts from the easternmost radio tower at Hull, charted in approximate position latitude 42°16.7' N., longitude 70°52.6' W., to Race Point on Cape Cod.

(b) A line drawn from Canal Breakwater Light 4 south to the shoreline.

§ 80.145 Race Point, MA to Watch Hill, Rl.

(a) Except inside lines specifically described in this section, the 72 COLREGS shall apply on the sounds, bays, harbors and inlets along the coast of Cape Cod and the southern coasts of Massachusetts and Rhode Island from Race Point to Watch Hill.

(b) A line drawn from Nobska Point Light to Tarpaulin Cove Light on the southeastern side of Naushon Island; thence from the southernmost tangent of Naushon Island to the easternmost extremity of Nashawena Island; thence from the southwestern most extremity of Nashawena Island to the easternmost extremity of Cuttyhunk Island; thence from the southwestern tangent of Cuttyhunk Island to the tower on Gooseberry Neck charted in approximate position latitude 41°29.1' N. longitude 71°02.3' W.

(c) A line drawn from Sakonnet Breakwater Light 2 tangent to the southernmost part of Sachuest Point charted in approximate position latitude 41° 28.5' N. longitude 71°14.8' W.

(d) An east-west line drawn through Beavertail Light between Brenton Point and the Boston Neck shoreline.

§ 80.150 Block Island, Rl.

The 72 COLREGS shall apply on the harbors of Block Island.

§ 80.155 Watch Hill, Rl to Montauk Point, NY.

(a) A line drawn from Watch Hill Light to East Point on Fishers Island.

(b) A line drawn from Race Point to Race Rock Light; thence to Little Gull Island Light thence to East Point on Plum Island.

(c) A line drawn from Plum Island Harbor East Dolphin Light to Plum Island Harbor West Dolphin Light.

(d) A line drawn from Plum Island Light to Orient Point Light; thence to Orient Point.

(e) A line drawn from the lighthouse ruins at the southwestern end of Long Beach Point to Cornelius Point.

(f) A line drawn from Coecles Harbor Entrance Light to Sungic Point.

(g) A line drawn from Nichols Point to Cedar Island Light.

(h) A line drawn from Three Mile Harbor West Breakwater Light to Three Mile Harbor East Breakwater Light.

(i) A line drawn from Montauk West Jetty Light 1 to Montauk East Jetty Light 2.

§ 80.160 Montauk Point, NY to Atlantic Beach, NY.

(a) A line drawn from Shinnecock Inlet East Breakwater Light to Shinnecock Inlet West Breakwater Light 1.

(b) A line drawn from Moriches Inlet East Breakwater Light to Moriches Inlet West Breakwater Light.

(c) A line drawn from Fire Island Inlet Breakwater Light 348° true to the southernmost extremity of the spit of land at the western end of Oak Beach.

(d) A line drawn from Jones Inlet Light 322° true across the southwest tangent of the island on the north side of Jones Inlet to the shoreline.

§ 80.165 New York Harbor.

A line drawn from East Rockaway Inlet Breakwater Light to Sandy Hook Light.

§ 80.170 Sandy Hook, NJ to Tom's River, NJ.

(a) A line drawn from Shark River Inlet North Breakwater Light 2 to Shark River Inlet South Breakwater Light 1.

(b) A line drawn from Manasquan Inlet North Breakwater Light 4 to Manasquan Inlet South Breakwater Light 3.

(c) A line drawn from Barnegat Inlet North Breakwater Light 4A to the seaward extremity of the submerged Barnegat Inlet South Breakwater; thence along the submerged breakwater to the shoreline.

§ 80.501 Tom's River, NJ to Cape May, NJ.

(a) A line drawn from the seaward tangent of Long Beach Island to the seaward tangent to Pullen Island across Beach Haven and Little Egg Inlets.

(b) A line drawn from the seaward tangent of Pullen Island to the seaward tangent of Brigantine Island across Brigantine Inlet.

(c) A line drawn from the seaward extremity of Absecon Inlet North Jetty to Atlantic City Light.

(d) A line drawn from the southernmost point of Longport at latitude 39°18.2' N. longitude 74°33.1'W. to the northeasternmost point of Ocean City at latitude 39°17.6' N. longitude 74° 33.1'W. across Great Egg Harbor Inlet.

(e) A line drawn parallel with the general trend of highwater shoreline across Corson Inlet.

(f) A line formed by the centerline of the Townsend Inlet Highway Bridge.

(g) A line formed by the shoreline of Seven Mile Beach and Hereford Inlet Light.

(h) A line drawn from Cape May Inlet East Jetty Light to Cape May Inlet West Jetty Light.

§ 80.503 Delaware Bay.

A line drawn from Cape May Light to Harbor of Refuge Light; thence to the northernmost extremity of Cape Henlopen.

§ 80.505 Cape Henlopen, DE to Cape Charles, VA.

(a) A line drawn from the seaward extremity of Indian River Inlet North Jetty to Indian River Inlet South Jetty Light.

(b) A line drawn from Ocean City Inlet Light 6 225° true across Ocean City Inlet to the submerged south breakwater.

(c) A line drawn from Assateague Beach Tower Light to the tower charted at latitude 37°52.6' N. longitude 75°26.7'W.

(d) A line formed by the range of Wachapreague Inlet Light 3 and Parramore Beach Lookout Tower drawn across Wachapreague Inlet.

(e) A line drawn from the lookout tower charted on the northern end of Hog Island to the seaward tangent of ParramoreBeach.

(f) A Line drawn 207° true from the lookout tower charted on the southern end of Hog Island across Great Machipongo Inlet

(g) A line formed by the range of the two cupolas charted on the southern end of Cobb Island drawn across Sand Shoal Inlet.

(h) Except as provided elsewhere in this section from Cape Henlopen to Cape Charles, lines drawn parallel with the general trend of the highwater shoreline across the entrances to small bays and inlets.

§ 80.510 Chesapeake Bay Entrance, VA.

A line drawn from Cape Charles Light to Cape Henry Light.

§ 80.515 Cape Henry, VA to Cape Hatteras, NC.

(a) A line drawn from Rudee Inlet Jetty Light 2 to Rudee Inlet Jetty Light 1.

(b) A line formed by the centerline of the highway bridge across Oregon Inlet.

§ 80.520 Cape Hatteras, NC to Cape Lookout, NC.

(a) A line drawn from Hatteras Inlet Lookout Tower at latitude 35°11.8' N. longitude 75°44.9'W 255° true to the eastern end of Ocracoke Island.

(b) A line drawn from the westernmost extremity of Ocracoke Island at latitude 35°04.0' N. longitude 76°00.8'W. to the northeastern extremity of Portsmouth Island at latitude 35°03.7' N. longitude 76°02.3'W.

(c) A line drawn across Drum Inlet parallel with the general trend of the highwater shoreline.

§ 80.525 Cape Lookout, NC to Cape Fear, NC.

(a) A line drawn from Cape Lookout Light to the seaward tangent of the southeastern end of Shackleford Banks.

(b) A line drawn from Morehead City Channel Range Front Light to the seaward extremity of the Beaufort Inlet west jetty.

(c) A line drawn from the southernmost extremity of Bogue Banks at latitude 34°38.7' N. longitude 77°06.0'W. across Bogue Inlet to the northernmost extremity

of Bear Beach at latitude 34°
38.5' N. longitude 77°07.1' W.
(d) A line drawn from the tower
charted in approximate position
latitude 34°31.5' N. longitude 77°
20.8' W. to the seaward tangent
of the shoreline on the northeast
side of New River Inlet.
(e) A line drawn across New
Topsail Inlet between the closest
extremities of the shore on either
side of the inlet from latitude 34°
20.8' N. longitude 77°39.2' W. to
latitude 34°20.6' N. longitude 77°
39.6' W.
(f) A line drawn from the seaward
extremity of the jetty on the
northeast side of Masonboro
Inlet to the seaward extremity of
the jetty on the southeast side
of the Inlet.
(g) Except as provided elsewhere
in this section from Cape
Lookout to Cape Fear, lines
drawn parallel with the general
trend of the highwater shoreline
across the entrance of small
bays and inlets.

§ 80.530 Cape Fear, NC to Little River Inlet, NC.

(a) A line drawn from the abandoned
lighthouse charted in
approximate position latitude 33°
52.4'N. longitude 78°00.1'W.
across the Cape Fear River
Entrance to Oak Island Light.
(b) Except as provided elsewhere
in this section from Cape
Fear to Little River Inlet, lines
drawn parallel with the general
trend of the highwater shoreline
across the entrance to small
inlets.

§ 80.703 Little River Inlet, SC to Cape Romain, SC.

(a) A line drawn from the westernmost extremity of the sand
spit on Bird Island to the easternmost
extremity of Waties Island across Little
River Inlet.
(b) From Little River Inlet, a
line drawn parallel with the general
trend of the highwater
shoreline across Hog Inlet;
thence a line drawn from Murrels
Inlet Light 2 to Murrels Inlet Light
1; thence a line drawn parallel
with the general trend of the
highwater shoreline across
Midway Inlet, Pawleys Inlet and
North Inlet.
(c) A line drawn from the charted
position of Winyah Bay North
Jetty End Buoy 2N south to the
Winyah Bay South Jetty.
(d) A line drawn from Santee
Point to the seaward tangent of
Cedar Island.
(e) A line drawn from Cedar
Island Point west to Murphy
Island.
(f) A north-south line (longitude
79°20.3' W.) drawn from Murphy
Island to the northernmost
extremity of Cape Island Point.

§ 80.707 Cape Romain, SC to Sullivans Island, SC.

(a) A line drawn from the western
extremity of Cape Romain
292° true to Racoon Key on the
west side of Racoon Creek.
(b) A line drawn from the westernmost extremity of Sandy

Point across Bull Bay to the northernmost extremity of Northeast Point.

(c) A line drawn from the southernmost extremity of Bull Island to the easternmost extremity of Capers Island.

(d) A line formed by the overhead power cable from Capers Island to Dewees Island.

(e) A line formed by the overhead power cable from Dewees Island to Isle of Palms.

(f) A line formed by the centerline of the highway bridge between Isle of Palms and Sullivans Island over Breach Inlet.

§ 80.710 Charleston Harbor, SC.

(a) A line formed by the submerged north jetty from theshore to the west end of the north jetty.

(b) A line drawn from across the seaward extremity of the Charleston Harbor Jetties.

(c) A line drawn from the west end of the South Jetty across the South Entrance to Charleston Harbor to shore on a line formed by the submerged south jetty.

§ 80.712 Morris Island, SC to Hilton Head Island, SC.

(a) A line drawn from the easternmost tip of Folly Island to the abandoned lighthouse tower on the northside of Lighthouse Inlet; thence west to the shoreline of Morris Island.

(b) A straight line drawn from the seaward tangent of Folly Island through Folly River Daybeacon 10 across Stono River to the shoreline of Sandy Point.

(c) A line drawn from the southernmost extremity of Seabrook Island 257° true across the North Edisto River Entrance to the shore of Botany Bay Island.

(d) A line drawn from the microwave antenna tower on Edisto Beach charted in approximate position latitude 32°29.3' N. longitude 80°19.2' W. across St. Helena Sound to the abandoned lighthouse tower on Hunting Island.

(e) A line formed by the centerline of the highway bridge between Hunting Island and Fripp Island.

(f) A line drawn from the westernmost extremity of Bull Point on Capers Island to Port Royal Sound Channel Range Rear Light, latitude 32°13.7' N. longitude 80°36.0' W.; thence 259° true to the easternmost extremity of Hilton Head at latitude 32°13.7' N. longitude 80°40.1' W.

§ 80.715 Savannah River.

A line drawn from the southernmost tank on Hilton Head Island charted in approximate position latitude 32°06.7' N. longitude 80°49.3' W. to Bloody Point Range Rear Light; thence to Tybee (Range Rear) Light.

§ 80.717 Tybee Island, GA to St. Simons Island, GA.

(a) A line drawn from the southernmost extremity of Savannah Beach on Tybee Island 255° true across Tybee Inlet to the shore of Little Tybee Island south of the entrance to Buck Hammock Creek.

(b) A straight line drawn from the northeasternmost extremity of Wassaw Island 031° true through Tybee River Daybeacon 1 to the shore of Little Tybee Island.

(c) A line drawn approximately parallel with the general trend of the highwater shorelines from the seaward tangent of Wassau Island to the seaward tangent of Bradley Point on Ossabaw Island.

(d) A north-south line (longitude 81°08.4'W.) drawn from the south-ernmost extremity of Ossabaw Island to St. Catherines Island.

(e) A north-south line (longitude 81°10.6'W.) drawn from the southernmost extremity of St. Catherines Island to North-east Point on Blackbeard Island.

(f) A line following the general trend of the seaward highwater shoreline across Cabretta Inlet.

(g) A north-south line (longitude 81°16.9'W.) drawn from the southwesternmost point on Sapelo Island to Wolf Island.

(h) A north-south line (longitude 81°17.1'W.) drawn from the southeasternmost point of Wolf Island to the northeasternmost point on Little St. Simons Island.

(i) A line drawn from the northeast-ernmost extremity of Sea Island 045° true to Little St. Simons Island.

(j) An east-west line from the southernmost extremity of Sea Island across Goulds Inlet to St. Simons Island.

§ 80.720 St. Simons Island, GA to Amelia Island, FL.

(a) A line drawn from St. Simons Light to the northernmost tank on Jekyll Island charted in approximate position latitude 31°05.9' N. longitude 81° 24.5'W.

(b) A line drawn from the southernmost tank on Jekyll Island charted in approximate position latitude 31°01.6' N. longitude 81°25.2'W. to coordinate latitude 30°59.4'N. longitude 81°23.7'W. (0.5 nautical mile east of the charted position of St. Andrew Sound Lighted Buoy 32); thence to the abandoned lighthouse tower on the north end of Little Cumberland Island charted in approximate position latitude 30°58.5'N. longitude 81°24.8'W.

(c) A line drawn across the seaward extremity of the St. Marys Entrance Jetties.

§80.723 Amelia Island, FL to Cape Canaveral, FL.

(a) A line drawn from the southern-most extremity of Amelia Island to the northeasternmost extremity of Little Talbot Island.

(b) A line formed by the centerline of the highway bridge from Little Talbot Island to Fort George Island.

(c) A line drawn across the seaward extremity of the St. Johns River Entrance Jetties.

(d) A line drawn across the seaward extremity of the St. Augustine Inlet Jetties.

(e) A line formed by the centerline of the highway bridge over

Matanzas Inlet.

(f) A line drawn across the seaward extremity of the Ponce de Leon Inlet Jetties.

§ 80.727 Cape Canaveral, FL to Miami Beach, FL.

(a) A line drawn across the seaward extremity of the Port Canaveral Entrance Channel Jetties.

(b) A line drawn across the seaward extremity of the Sebastian Inlet Jetties.

(c) A line drawn across the seaward extremity of the Fort Pierce Inlet Jetties.

(d) A north-south line (longitude 80° 09.7' W.) drawn across St. Lucie Inlet.

(e) A line drawn from the seaward extremity of Jupiter inlet North Jetty to the northeast extremity of the concrete apron on the south side of Jupiter inlet.

(f) A line drawn across the seaward extremity of the Lake Worth Inlet Jetties.

(g) A line drawn across the seaward extremity of the Boynton Inlet Jetties.

(h) A line drawn from Boca Raton Inlet North Jetty Light 2 to Boca Raton Inlet South Jetty Light 1.

(i) A line drawn from Hillsboro Inlet Light to Hillsboro Inlet Entrance Light 2; thence to Hillsboro Inlet Entrance Light 1; thence west to the shoreline.

(j) A line drawn across the seaward extremity of the Port Everglades Entrance Jetties.

(k) A line formed by the centerline of the highway bridge over Bakers Haulover Inlet.

§ 80.730 Miami Harbor, FL.

A line drawn across the seaward extremity of the Miami Harbor Government Cut Jetties.

§ 80.735 Miami, FL to Long Key, FL.

(a) A line drawn from the southernmost extremity of Fisher Island 212° true to the point latitude 25°45.0' N. longitude 80° 08.6' W. on Virginia Key.

(b) A line formed by the centerline of the highway bridge between Virginia Key and Key Biscayne.

(c) A line drawn from Cape Florida Light to the northernmost extremity on Soldier Key.

(d) A line drawn from the southernmost extremity on Soldier Key to the northernmost extremity of the Ragged Keys.

(e) A line drawn from the Ragged Keys to the southernmost extremity of Angelfish Key following the general trend of the seaward shoreline.

(f) A line drawn on the centerline of the Overseas Highway (U.S. 1) and bridges from latitude 25°19.3' N. longitude 80° 16.0' W. at Little Angelfish Creek to the radar dome charted on Long Key at approximate position latitude 24°49.3' N. longitude 80°49.2' W.

PUERTO RICO AND VIRGIN ISLANDS

SEVENTH DISTRICT

§ 80.738 Puerto Rico and Virgin Islands.

(a) Except inside lines specifically

described in this section, the 72 COLREGS shall apply on all other bays, harbors and lagoons of Puerto Rico and the U.S. Virgin Islands.

(b) A line drawn from Puerto San Juan Light to Cabras Light across the entrance of San Juan Harbor.

GULF COAST

SEVENTH DISTRICT

§80.740 Long Key, FL to Cape Sable, FL.

A line drawn from the microwave tower charted on Long Key at approximate position latitude 24° 48.8' N. longitude 80° 49.6' W. to Long Key Light 1; thence to Arsenic Bank Light 2; thence to Sprigger Bank Light 5; thence to Schooner Bank Light 6; thence to Oxfoot Bank Light 10; thence to East Cape Light 2; thence through East Cape Daybeacon 1A to the shoreline at East Cape.

§ 80.745 Cape Sable, FL to Cape Romano, FL.

(a) A line drawn following the general trend of the mainland, highwater shoreline from Cape Sable at East Cape to Little Shark River Light 1; thence to westernmost extremity of Shark Point; thence following the general trend of the mainland, highwater shoreline crossing the entrances of Harney River, Broad Creek, Broad River, Rodgers River First Bay, Chatham River, Huston River, to the shoreline at coordinate latitude 25°41.8' N. longitude 81°17.9'W.

(b) The 72 COLREGS shall apply to the waters surrounding the Ten Thousand Islands and the bays, creeks, inlets, and rivers between Chatham Bend and Marco Island except inside lines specifically described in this part.

(c) A north-south line drawn at longitude 81°20.2' W. across the entrance to Lopez River.

(d) A line drawn across the entrance to Turner River parallel to the general trend of the shoreline.

(e) A line formed by the centerline of Highway 92 Bridge at Goodland.

§ 80.748 Cape Romano, FL to Sanibel Island, FL.

(a) A line drawn across Big Marco Pass parallel to the general trend of the seaward, highwater shoreline.

(b) A line drawn from the northwesternmost extremity of Coconut Island 000°T across Capri Pass.

(c) Lines drawn across Hurricane and Little Marco Passes parallel to the general trend of the seaward, highwater shoreline.

(d) A line from the seaward extremity of Gordon Pass South Jetty 014° true to the shoreline at approximate coordinate latitude 26°05.7' N. longitude 81°48.1' W.

(e) A line drawn across the seaward extremity of Doctors Pass Jetties.

(f) Lines drawn across Wiggins, Big Hickory, New, and Big Carlos Passes parallel to the general trend of the seaward highwater shoreland.

(g) A straight line drawn from Sanibel Island Light through Matanzas Pass Channel Light 2 to the shore of Estero Island.

§ 80.750 Sanibel Island, FL to St. Petersburg, FL.

(a) A line formed by the centerline of the highway bridge over Blind Pass, between Captiva Island and Sanibel Island, and lines drawn across Redfish and Captiva Passes parallel to the general trend of the seaward, highwater shorelines.

(b) A line drawn from La Costa Test Pile North Light to Port Boca Grande Light.

(c) Lines drawn across Gasparilla and Stump Passes parallel to the general trend of the seaward, highwater shorelines.

(d) A line across the seaward extremity of Venice Inlet Jetties.

(e) A line drawn across Midnight Pass parallel to the general trend of the seaward, highwater shoreline.

(f) A line drawn from Big Sarasota Pass Light 14 to the southernmost extremity of Lido Key.

(g) A line drawn across New Pass tangent to the seaward, highwater shoreline of Longboat Key.

(h) A line drawn across Longboat Pass parallel to the seaward, highwater shoreline.

(i) A line drawn from the northwesternmost extremity of Bean Point to the southeasternmost extremity of Egmont Key.

(j) A straight line drawn from Egmont Key Light through Egmont Channel Range Rear Light to the shoreline on Mullet Key.

(k) A line drawn from the northernmost extremity of Mullet Key across Bunces Pass and South Channel to Pass-a-Grille Channel Light 8; thence to Pass-a-Grille Channel Daybeacon 9; thence to the southwesternmost extremity of Long Key.

§ 80.753 St. Petersburg, FL to Anclote, FL.

(a) A line drawn across Blind Pass, between Treasure Island and Long Key, parallel with the general trend of the seaward, highwater shoreline.

(b) Lines formed by the centerline of the highway bridges over Johns and Clearwater Passes.

(c) A line drawn across Dunedin and Hurricane Passes parallel with the general trend of the seaward, highwater shoreline.

(d) A line drawn from the northernmost extremity of Honeymoon Island to Anclote Anchorage South Entrance Light 7; thence to Anclote Key 28° 10.0' N 82°50.6' W; thence a straight line through Anclote River Cut B Range Rear Light to the shoreline.

§ 80.755 Anclote, FL to the Suncoast Keys, FL.

(a) Except inside lines specifically described in this section, the 72 COLREGS shall apply on the bays, bayous, creeks, marinas, and rivers from Anclote to the Suncoast Keys.

(b) A north-south line drawn at longitude 82°38.3' W. across the Chassahowitzka River Entrance.

§ 80.757 Suncoast Keys, FL to Horseshoe Point, FL.

(a) Except inside lines specifically described in this section, the 72 COLREGS shall apply on the bays, bayous, creeks, and marinas from the Suncoast Keys to Horseshoe Point.

(b) A line formed by the centerline of Highway 44 Bridge over the Salt River.

(c) A north-south line drawn through Crystal River Entrance Daybeacon 25 across the river entrance.

(d) A north-south line drawn through the Cross Florida Barge Canal Daybeacon 48 across the canal.

(e) A north-south line drawn through Withlacoochee River Daybeacon 40 across the river.

(f) A line drawn from the western-most extremity of South Point north to the shoreline across the Waccasassa River Entrance.

(g) A line drawn from position latitude 29°16.6' N. longitude 83°06.7' W. 300° true to the shoreline of Hog Island.

(h) A north-south line drawn through Suwannee River Wadley Pass Channel Daybeacons 30 and 31 across the Suwannee River.

§ 80.760 Horseshoe Point, FL to Rock Islands, FL.

(a) Except inside lines specifically described provided in this section, the 72 COLREGS shall apply on the bays, bayous, creeks, marinas, and rivers from Horseshoe Point to the Rock Islands.

(b) A north-south line drawn through Steinhatchee River Light 21.

(c) A line drawn from Fenholloway River Approach Light FR east across the entrance to Fenholloway River.

EIGHTH DISTRICT

§ 80.805 Rock Island, FL to Cape San Blas, FL.

(a) A north-south line drawn from the Econfina River Light to the opposite shore.

(b) A line drawn from Gamble Point Light to the southernmost extremity of Cabell Point.

(c) A line drawn from St. Marks (Range Rear) Light to St. Marks Channel Light 11; thence to the southernmost extremity of Live Oak Point; thence in a straight line through Shell Point Light to the southernmost extremity of Ochlockonee Point; thence to Bald Point along longitude 84° 20.5' W.

(d) A line drawn from the south shore of Southwest Cape at longitude 84°22.7' W. to Dog Island Reef East Light 1; thence to Turkey Point Light 2; thence to the easternmost extremity of Dog Island.

(e) A line drawn from the western-most extremity of Dog Island to the easternmost extremity of St. George Island.

(f) A line drawn across the seaward extremity of the St. George Island Channel Jetties.

(g) A line drawn from the northwest-

ernmost extremity of Sand
Island to West Pass Light 7.

(h) A line drawn from the western-
mostextremity of St. VincenT
Island to the southeast, highwater
shoreline of Indian Peninsula
at longitude 85°13.5' W.

§ 80.810 Cape San Blas, FL to Perdido Bay, FL.

(a) A line drawn from St.
Joseph Bay Entrance Range A
Rear Light through St. Joseph
Bay Entrance Range B Front
Light to St. Joseph Point.

(b) A line drawn across the
mouth of Salt Creek as an extension
of the general trend of the
shoreline to continue across the
inlet to St. Andrews Sound in the
middle of Crooked Island.

(c) A line drawn from the northern-
mostextremity of Crooked
Island 000°T. to the mainland.

(d) A line drawn from the easternmost extremity of Shell Island
120° true to the shoreline across
the east entrance to St. Andrews
Bay.

(e) A line drawn between the
seaward end of the St. Andrews
Bay Entrance Jetties.

(f) A line drawn between the
seaward end of the Choctawatchee
Bay Entrance Jetties.

(g) A east-west line drawn from
Fort McRee Leading Light
across the Pensacola Bay
Entrance along latitude 30°19.5'
N.

(h) A line drawn between the
seaward end of the Perdido
Pass Jetties.

§ 80.815 Mobile Bay, AL to the Chandeleur Islands, LA.

(a) A line drawn across the inlets
to Little Lagoon as an extension
of the general trend of the
shoreline.

(b) A line drawn from Mobile
Point Light to Dauphin Island
Channel Light No. 1 to the eastern
corner of Fort Gaines at
Pelican Point.

(c) A line drawn from the westernmost extremity of Dauphin
Island to the easternmost
extremity of Petit Bois Island.

(d) A line drawn from Horn
Island Pass Entrance Range
Front Light on Petit Bois Island
to the easternmost extremity of
Horn Island.

(e) An east-west line (latitude
30°14.7' N.) drawn between the
westernmost extremity of Horn
Island to the easternmost extremity
of Ship Island.

(f) A curved line drawn following
the general trend of the seaward,
highwater shoreline of
Ship Island.

(g) A line drawn from Ship
Island Light to Chandeleur Light;
thence in a curved line following
the general trend of the seaward,
highwater shorelines of the
Chandeleur Islands to the
island at latitude 29°44.1' N. longitude 88°53.0' W.; thence to
latitude 29°26.5'N. longitude 88°
55.6'W.

§ 80.825 Mississippi Passes, LA.

(a) A line drawn from latitude
29°26.5'N., longitude 88°55.6'W.
to latidude 29°10.6'N., longitude

88°59.8'W.; thence to latitude 29°03.5'N., longitude 89°03.7'W.; thence to latitude 28°58.8'N., longitude 89°04.3'W.

(b) A line drawn from latitude 28°58.8'N., longitude 89°04.3'W.; to latitude 28°57.3'N., longitude 89°05.3'W.; thence to latitude 28°56.95'N., longitude 89°05.6'W.; thence to latitude 29°00.4'N., longitude 89°09.8'W.; thence following the general trend of the seaward highwater shoreline in a northwesterly direction to latitude 29°03.4'N., longitude 89°13.0'W.; thence west to latitude 29°03.5'N., longitude 89°15.5'W.; thence following the general trend of the seaward highwater shoreline in a southwesterly direction to latitude 28°57.7'N., longitude 89°22.3'W.

(c) A line drawn from latitude 28°57.7'N., longitude 89°22.3'W.; to latitude 28°51.4'N., longitude 89°24.5'W.; thence to latitude 28°52.65'N., longitude 89°27.1'W.; thence to the seaward extremity of the Southwest Pass West Jetty located at latitude 28°54.5'N., longitude 89°26.1'W.

(d) A line drawn from Mississippi River South Pass East Jetty Light 4 to Mississippi River South Pass West Jetty Light; thence following the general trend of the seaward highwater shoreline in a northwesterly direction to coordinate latitude 29°03.4'N. longitude 89°13.0'W.; thence west to coordinate latitude 29°03.5'N., longitude 89°15.5'W., thence following the general trend of the seaward, highwater shoreline in a southwesterly direction to Mississippi River Southwest Pass Entrance Light.

(e) A line drawn from Mississippi River Southwest Pass Entrance Light; thence to the seaward extremity of the Southwest Pass West Jetty located at coordinate latitude 28°54.5'N. longitude 89°26.1'W.

§ 80.830 Mississippi Passes, LA to Point Au Fer, LA.

(a) A line drawn from the seaward extremity of the Southwest Pass West Jetty located at coordinate latitude 28°54.5'N. longitude 89°26.1'W.; thence following the general trend of the seaward, highwater jetty and shoreline in a north, northeasterly direction to Old Tower latitude 28°58.8'N. longitude 89°23.3'W.; thence to West Bay Light; thence to coordinate latitude 29°05.2'N. longitude 89°24.3'W.; thence a curved line following the general trend of the highwater shoreline to Point Au Fer Island except as otherwise described in this section.

(b) A line drawn across the seaward extremity of the Empire Waterway (Bayou Fontanelle) entrance jetties.

(c) An east-west line drawn from the westernmost extremity of Grand Terre Islands in the direction of 194° true to the Grand Isle Fishing Jetty Light.

(d) A line drawn between the seaward extremity of the Belle Pass Jetties.

(e) A line drawn from the westernmost extremity of the Timbalier Island to the easternmost extremity of Isles Dernieres.

(f) A north-south line drawn from Caillou Bay Light 13 across Caillou Boca.

(g) A line drawn 107° true from Caillou Bay Boat Landing Light across the entrances to Grand Bayou du Large and Bayou Grand Caillou.

(h) A line drawn on an axis of 103° true through Taylors Bayou Entrance Light 2 across the entrances to Jack Stout Bayou, Taylors Bayou, Pelican Pass, and Bayou de West.

§ 80.835 Point Au Fer, LA to Calcasieu Pass, LA.

(a) A line drawn from Point Au Fer to Atchafalaya Channel Light 34; thence to Point Au Fer Reef Light 33; thence to Atchafalaya Bay Pipeline Light D latitude 29°25.0'N. longitude 91°31.7'W.; thence to Atchafalaya Bay Light 1 latitude 29°25.3'N. longitude 91°35.8'W.; thence to South Point.

(b) Lines following the general trend of the highwater shoreline drawn across the bayou and canal inlets from the Gulf of Mexico between South Point and Calcasieu Pass except as otherwise described in this section.

(c) A line drawn on an axis of 140° true through Southwest Pass Vermillion Bay Light 4 across Southwest Pass.

(d) A line drawn across the seaward extremity of the Freshwater Bayou Canal Entrance Jetties.

(e) A line drawn from Mermentau Channel East Jetty Light 6 to Mermentau Channel West Jetty Light 7.

(f) A line drawn from the radio tower charted in approximate position latitude 29°45.7'N. longitude 93°06.3'W. 115° true across Mermentau Pass.

(g) A line drawn across the seaward extremity of the Calcasieu Pass Jetties.

§ 80.840 Sabine Pass, TX to Galveston, TX.

(a) A line drawn from the Sabine Pass East Jetty Light to the seaward end of the Sabine Pass West Jetty.

(b) A line drawn across the small boat passes through the Sabine Pass East and West Jetties.

(c) A line formed by the centerline of the highway bridge over Rollover Pass at Gilchrist.

§ 80.845 Galveston, TX to Freeport, TX.

(a) A line drawn from Galveston North Jetty Light 6A to Galveston South Jetty Light 5A.

(b) A line formed by the centerline of the highway bridge over San Luis Pass.

(c) Lines formed by the centerlines of the highway bridges over the inlets to Christmas Bay (Cedar Cut) and Drum Bay.

(d) A line drawn from the seaward extremity of the Freeport North Jetty to Freeport Entrance Light 6; thence to Freeport Entrance Light 7; thence to the seaward extremity of Freeport South Jetty.

§ 80.850 Brazos River, TX to the Rio Grande, TX.

(a) Except as otherwise described in this section lines drawn continuing the general trend of the seaward, highwater shorelines across the inlets to Brazos River Diversion Channel, San Bernard River, Cedar Lakes, Brown Cedar Cut, Colorado River, Matagorda Bay, Cedar Bayou, Corpus Christi Bay, and Laguna Madre.

(b) A line drawn across the seaward extremity of Matagorda Ship Channel North Jetties.

(c) A line drawn from the seaward tangent of Matagorda Peninsula at Decros Point to Matagorda Light.

(d) A line drawn across the seaward extremity of the Aransas Pass Jetties.

(e) A line drawn across the seaward extremity of the Port Mansfield Entrance Jetties.

(f) A line drawn across the seaward extremity of the Brazos Santiago Pass Jetties.

PACIFIC COAST

ELEVENTH DISTRICT

§ 80.1102 Santa Catalina Island, CA.

The 72 COLREGS shall apply to the harbors on Santa Catalina Island.

§ 80.1104 San Diego Harbor, CA.

A line drawn from Zuniga Jetty Light "V" to Zuniga Jetty Light "Z"; thence to Point Loma Light.

§ 80.1106 Mlssion Bay, CA.

A line drawn from Mission Bay South Jetty Light 2 to Mission Bay North Jetty Light 1.

§ 80.1108 Oceanside Harbor, CA.

A line drawn from Oceanside South Jetty Light 4 to Oceanside Breakwater Light 3.

§ 80.1110 Dana Point Harbor, CA.

A line drawn from Dana Point Jetty Light 6 to Dana Point Breakwater Light 5.

§ 80.1112 Newport Bay, CA.

A line drawn from Newport Bay East Jetty Light 4 to Newport Bay West Jetty Light 3.

§ 80.1114 San Pedro Bay–Anaheim Bay, CA.

(a) A line drawn across the seaward extremities of the Anaheim Bay Entrance East Jetties; thence to Long Beach Breakwater East End Light 1.

(b) A line drawn from Long Beach Channel Entrance Light 2 to Long Beach Light.

(c) A line drawn from Los Angeles Main Entrance Channel Light 2 to Los Angeles Light.

§ 80.1116 Redondo Harbor, CA.

A line drawn from Redondo Beach East Jetty Light 2 to Redondo Beach West Jetty Light 3.

§ 80.1118 Marina Del Rey, CA.

(a) A line drawn from Marina Del Rey Breakwater South Light 1 to Marina Del Rey Light 4.

(b) A line drawn from Marina Del Rey Breakwater North Light 2 to Marina Del Rey Light 3.

(c) A line drawn from Marina Del Rey Light 4 to the seaward extremity of the Ballona Creek South Jetty.

§ 80.1120 Port Hueneme, CA.

A line drawn from Port Hueneme East Jetty Light 4 to Port Hueneme West Jetty Light 3.

§ 80.1122 Channel Islands Harbor, CA.

(a) A line drawn from Channel Islands Harbor South Jetty Light 2 to Channel Islands Harbor Breakwater South Light 1.

(b) A line drawn from Channel Islands Harbor Breakwater North Light to Channel Islands Harbor North Jetty Light 5.

§ 80.1124 Ventura Marina, CA.

A line drawn from Ventura Marina South Jetty Light 6 to Ventura Marina Breakwater South Light 3; thence to Ventura Marina North Jetty Light 7.

§ 80.1126 Santa Barbara Harbor, CA.

A line drawn from Santa Barbara Harbor Light 4 to Santa Barbara Harbor Breakwater Light.

§ 80.1130 San Luis Obispo Bay, CA.

A line drawn from the southernmost extremity of Fossil Point to the seaward extremity of Whaler Island Breakwater.

§ 80.1132 Estero-Morro Bay, CA.

A line drawn from the seaward extremity of the Morro Bay East Breakwater to the Morro Bay West Breakwater Light.

§ 80.1134 Monterey Harbor, CA.

A line drawn from Monterey Harbor Light 6 to the northern extremity of Monterey Municipal Wharf 2.

§ 80.1136 Moss Landing Harbor, CA.

A line drawn from the seaward extremity of the pier located 0.3 mile south of Moss Landing Harbor Entrance to the seaward extremity of the Moss Landing Harbor North Breakwater.

§ 80.1138 Santa Cruz Harbor, CA.

A line drawn from the seaward extremity of the Santa Cruz Harbor East Breakwater to Santa Cruz Harbor West Breakwater Light; thence to Santa Cruz Light.

§ 80.1140 Pillar Point Harbor, CA.

A line drawn from Pillar Point Harbor Light 6 to Pillar Point Harbor Entrance Light.

§ 80.1142 San Francisco Harbor, CA.

A straight line drawn from Point Bonita Light through Mile Rocks Light to the shore.

§ 80.1144 Bodega and Tomales Bay, CA.

(a) An east-west line drawn from Sand Point to Avalis Beach.
(b) A line drawn from the seaward extremity of Bodega Harbor North Breakwater to Bodega Harbor Entrance Light 1.

§ 80.1146 Albion River, CA.

A line drawn on an axis of 030° true through Albion River Light 1 across Albion Cove.

§ 80.1148 Noyo River, CA.

A line drawn from Noyo River Entrance Daybeacon 4 to Noyo River Entrance Light 5.

§ 80.1150 Arcata-Humboldt Bay, CA.

A line drawn from Humboldt Bay Entrance Light 4 to Humboldt Bay Entrance Light 3.

§ 80.1152 Crescent City Harbor, CA.

A line drawn from Crescent City Entrance Light to the southeast-ernmost extremity of Whaler Island.

THIRTEENTH DISTRICT

§ 80.1305 Chetco River, OR.

A line drawn across the seaward extremities of the Chetco River Entrance Jetties.

§ 80.1310 Rogue River, OR.

A line drawn across the seaward extremities of the Rogue River Entrance Jetties.

§ 80.1315 Coquille River, OR.

A line drawn across the seaward extremities of the Coquille River Entrance Jetties.

§ 80.1320 Coos Bay, OR.

A line drawn across the seaward extremities of the Coos Bay Entrance Jetties.

§ 80.1325 Umpqua River, OR.

A line drawn across the seaward extremities of the Umpqua Entrance Jetties.

§ 80.1330 Siuslaw River, OR.

A line drawn across the seaward extremities of the Siuslaw River Entrance Jetties.

§ 80.1335 Alsea Bay, OR.

A line drawn from the seaward shoreline on the north of the Alsea Bay Entrance 165° true across the channel entrance.

§ 80.1340 Yaquina Bay, OR.

A line drawn across the seaward extremities of Yaquina Bay Entrance Jetties.

§ 80.1345 Depoe Bay, OR.

A line drawn across the Depoe Bay Channel entrance parallel with the general trend of the highwater shoreline.

§ **80.1350 Netarts Bay, OR.**
A line drawn from the northernmost
extremity of the shore on
the south side of Netarts Bay
north to the opposite shoreline.

§ **80.1355 Tillamook Bay, OR.**
A line drawn across the seaward
extremities of the Tillamook
Bay Entrance Jetties.

§ **80.1360 Nehalem River, OR.**
A line drawn approximately
parallel with the general trend of
the highwater shoreline across
the Nehalem River Entrance.

§ **80.1365 Columbia River
Entrance, OR/WA.**
A line drawn from the seaward
extremity of the Columbia River
North Jetty (above water) 155°
true to the seaward extremity of
the Columbia River South Jetty
(above water).

§ **80.1370 Willapa Bay, WA.**
A line drawn from Willapa Bay
Light 169.8° true to the westernmost
tripod charted 1.6 miles
south of Leadbetter Point.

§ **80.1375 Grays Harbor, WA.**
A line drawn across the seaward
extremities (above water)
of the Grays Harbor Entrance
Jetties.

§ **80.1380 Quillayute River, WA.**
A line drawn from the seaward
extremity of the Quillayute River
Entrance East Jetty to the overhead
power cable tower charted
on James Island; thence a
straight line through Quillayute

River Entrance Light 3 to the
shoreline.

§ **80.1385 Strait of Juan de
Fuca.**
The 72 COLREGS shall apply
on all waters of the Strait of Juan
de Fuca.

§ **80.1390 Haro Strait and**
Strait of Georgia.
The 72 COLREGS shall apply
on all waters of the Haro Strait
and the Strait of Georgia.

§ **80.1395 Puget Sound and
Adjacent Waters.**
The 72 COLREGS shall apply
on all waters of Puget Sound
and adjacent waters, including
Lake Union, Lake Washington,
Hood Canal, and all tributaries.

PACIFIC ISLANDS
FOURTEENTH DISTRICT
§ **80.1410 Hawaiian Island**
Exemption from General Rule.
Except as provided elsewhere
in this part for Mamala Bay and
Kaneohe Bay on Oahu; Port
Allen and Nawiliwili Bay on
Kauai; Kahului Harbor on Maui;
and Kawailae and Hilo Harbors
on Hawaii, the 72 COLREGS
shall apply on all other bays, harbors,
and lagoons of theHawaiian
Island (including Midway).

§ **80.1420 Mamala Bay,
Oahu, HI.**
A line drawn from Barbers
Point Light to Diamond Head
Light.

§ 80.1430 Kaneohe Bay, Oahu, Hl.

A straight line drawn from Pyramid Rock Light across Kaneohe Bay through the center of Mokolii Island to the shoreline.

§ 80.1440 Port Allen, Kauai, Hl.

A line drawn from Hanapepe Light to Hanapepe Bay Breakwater Light.

§ 80.1450 Nawiliwili Harbor, Kauai, Hl.

A line drawn from Nawiliwili Harbor Breakwater Light to Kukii Point Light.

§ 80.1460 Kahului Harbor, Maui, Hl.

A line drawn from Kahului Harbor Entrance East Breakwater Light to Kahului Harbor Entrance West Breakwater Light.

§ 80.1470 Kawaihae Harbor, Hawaii, Hl.

A line drawn from Kawaihae Light to the seaward extremity of the Kawaihae South Breakwater.

§ 80.1480 Hilo Harbor, Hawaii, Hl.

A line drawn from the seaward extremity of the Hilo Breakwater 265° true (as an extension of the seaward side of the breakwater) to the shoreline 0.2 nautical mile north of Alealea Point.

§ 80.1490 Apra Harbor, U.S. Territory of Guam.

A line drawn from the westernmost extremity of Orote Island to the westernmost extremity of Glass Breakwater.

§ 80.1495 U.S. Pacific Island Possessions.

The 72 COLREGS shall apply on the bays, harbors, lagoons, and waters surrounding the U.S. Pacific Island Possessions of American Samoa, Baker, Howland, Jarvis, Johnson, Palmyra, Swains and Wake Island.

ALASKA

SEVENTEENTH DISTRICT

§ 80.1705 Alaska

The 72 COLREGS shall apply on all the sounds, bays, harbors, and inlets of Alaska.

PENALTY PROVISIONS

Other than laying out penalties and accident reporting procedures, this section details three important conditions that every recreational skipper should recognize. First, it calls for penalties for negligent boat operation. Second, it sets out the duty of everyone to provide assistance in the event of an accident. And, third, it relieves any skipper of liability who, in good faith and gratuitously, renders assistance at the scene of an accident in which he's involved. There is one proviso: such assistance must be given "without the objection by any individual being assisted." — The Editors

VIOLATIONS OF INTERNATIONAL NAVIGATION RULES AND REGULATIONS (33 U.S.C. 1608)

(a) Whoever operates a vessel, subject to the provisions of this Chapter, in violation of this Chapter or of any regulation promulgated pursuant to section 1607 of this title, shall be liable to a civil penalty of not more than $5,000 for each such violation.

(b) Every vessel subject to the provisions of this Chapter, other than a public vessel being used for noncommercial purposes, which is operated in violation of this Chapter or of any regulation promulgated pursuant to section 1607 of this title, shall be liable to a civil penalty of not more than $5,000 for each such violation, for which penalty the vessel may be seized and proceeded against in the district court of the United States of any district within which such vessel may be found.

(c) The Secretary of the department in which the Coast Guard is operating may assess any civil penalty authorized by this section. No such penalty may be assessed until the person charged, or the owner of the vessel charged, as appropriate, shall have been given notice of the violation involved and an opportunity for a hearing. For good cause shown, the Secretary may remit, mitigate, or compromise any penalty assessed. Upon the failure of the person charged, or the owner of the vessel charged, to pay an assessed penalty, as it may have been mitigated or compromised, the Secretary may request the Attorney General to commence an action in the appropriate district court of the United States for collection of the penalty as assessed, without regard to the amount involved, together with such other relief as may be appropriate.

VIOLATIONS OF INLAND NAVIGATION RULES AND REGULATIONS (33 U.S.C. 2072)

(a) Whoever operates a vessel in violation of this Chapter, or of any regulation issued thereunder, or in violation of a certificate of alternative

compliance issued under Rule 1 is liable to a civil penalty of not
more than $5,000 for each violation.

(b) Every vessel subject to this Chapter, other than a public vessel
being used for noncommercial purposes, that is operated in violation
of this Chapter, or of any regulation issued thereunder, or in violation
of a certificate of alternative compliance issued under Rule 1 is liable
to a civil penalty of not more than $5,000 for each violation, for which
penalty the vessel may be seized and proceeded against in the district
court of the United States of any district within which the vessel
may be found.

(c) The Secretary may assess any civil penalty authorized by this
section. No such penalty may be assessed until the person charged,
or the owner of the vessel charged, as appropriate, shall have been
given notice of the violation involved and an opportunity for a hearing.
For good cause shown, the Secretary may remit, mitigate, or
compromise any penalty assessed. Upon the failure of the person
charged, or the owner of the vessel charged, to pay an assessed
penalty, as it may have been mitigated or compromised, the
Secretary may request the Attorney General to commence an action
in the appropriate district court of the United States for collection of
the penalty as assessed, without regard to the amount involved,
together with such other relief as may be appropriate.

(d) (1) If any owner, operator, or individual in charge of a vessel is
liable for a penalty under this section, or if reasonable cause exists to
believe that the owner, operator, or individual in charge may be subject
to a penalty under this section, the Secretary of the Treasury,
upon the request of the Secretary, shall with respect to such vessel
refuse or revoke any clearance required by section 4197 of the
Revised Statutes of the United States (46 App. U.S.C. 91).

(2) Clearance or a permit refused or revoked under this subsection
may be granted upon filing of a bond or other surety satisfactory to
the Secretary.

PENALTIES FOR NEGLIGENT OPERATIONS; DUTIES RELATED TO MARINE CASUALTY ASSISTANCE AND INFORMATION; DUTY TO PROVIDE ASSISTANCE AT SEA; INJUNCTIONS (46 U.S.C. 2301-2305)

EXCERPT FROM TITLE 46 OF THE UNITED STATES CODE

CHAPTER 23—OPERATIONS OF VESSELS GENERALLY
[Enacted on August 26,1983]

§2301 Application

This chapter applies to a vessel operated on waters subject to the jurisdiction of the United States and, for a vessel owned in the United States, on the high seas.

§ 2302 Penalties for negligent operations

(a) A person operating a vessel in a negligent manner that endangers the life, limb, or property of a person is liable to the United States Government for a civil penalty of not more than $1,000.

(b) A person operating a vessel in a grossly negligent manner that endangers the life, limb, or property of a person shall be fined not more than $5,000, imprisoned for not more than one year, or both.

(c) An individual who is under the influence of alcohol, or a dangerous drug in violation of a law of the United States when operating a vessel, as determined under standards prescribed by the Secretary by regulation—

(1) is liable to the United States Government for a civil penalty of not more than $1,000 for a first violation and not more than $5,000 for a subsequent violation; or

(2) commits a class A misdemeanor.

(d) For a penalty imposed under this section, the vessel also is liable in rem unless the vessel is—

(1) owned by a State or a political subdivision of a State;

(2) operated principally for governmental purposes; and

(3) identified clearly as a vessel of that State or subdivision.

§ 2303 Duties related to marine casualty assistance and information

(a) The master or individual in charge of a vessel involved in a marine casualty shall—

(1) render necessary assistance to each individual affected to save that affected individual from danger caused by the marine casualty, so far as the master or individual in charge can do so without serious danger to the master's or individual's vessel or to individuals on board; and

(2) give the master's or individual's name and address and identification of the vessel to the master or individual in charge of any other vessel involved in the casualty, to any individual injured, and to the owner of any property damaged.

(b) An individual violating this section or a regulation prescribed under this section shall be fined not more than $1,000 or imprisoned for not more than 2 years. The vessel also is liable in rem to the United States Government for the fine.

(c) An individual complying with subsection (a) of this section or gratuitously and in good faith rendering assistance at the scene of a marine casualty without objection by an individual assisted, is not liable for damages as a result of rendering assistance or for an act or omission in providing or arranging salvage, towage, medical treatment, or other assistance when the individual acts as an ordinary, reasonable, and prudent individual would have acted under the circum stances.

§2304 Duty to provide assistance at sea

(a) A master or individual in charge of a vessel shall render assistance to any individual found at sea in danger of being lost, so far as the master or individual in charge can do so without serious danger to the master's or individual's vessel or individuals on board.

(b) A master or individual violating this section shall be fined not more than $1,000, imprisoned for not more than 2 years, or both.

§ 2305 Injunctions

(a) The district courts of the United States have jurisdiction to enjoin the negligent operation of vessels prohibited by this chapter on the petition of the Attorney General for the United States Government.

(b) When practicable, the Secretary shall—

(1) give notice to any person against whom an action for injunctive relief is considered under this section an opportunity to present that person's views; and

(2) except for a knowing and willful violation, give the person a reasonable opportunity to achieve compliance.

(c) The failure to give notice and opportunity to present views under subsection (b) of this section does not preclude the court from granting appropriate relief.

§ 2306 Vessel Reporting Requirements

(a)(1) An owner, charterer, managing operator, or agent of a vessel of the United States, having reason to believe (because of lack of communication with or nonappearance of a vessel or any other incident) that the vessel may have been lost or imperiled, immediately shall—

(A) notify the Coast Guard; and

(B) use all available means to determine the status of the vessel.

(2) When more than 48 hours have passed since the owner, charterer, managing operator, or agent of a vessel required to report to the United States Flag Merchant Vessel Location Filing System under authority of section 212 (A) of the Merchant Marine Act, 1936 (46 App. U. S. C. 1122a), has received a communication from the vessel, the owner, charterer, managing operator, or agent immediately shall—

(A) notify the Coast Guard; and

(B) use all available means to determine the status of the vessel.

(3) A person notifying the Coast Guard under paragraph (1) or (2) of this subsection shall provide the name and identification number of the vessel, the names of individuals on board, and other information that may be requested by the Coast Guard. The owner, charterer, managing operator, or agent also shall submit written confirmation to the Coast Guard 24 hours after nonwritten notification to the Coast Guard under those paragraphs.

(4) An owner, charterer, managing operator, or agent violating this subsection is liable to the United States Government for a civil penalty of not more than $5,000 for each day during which the violation occurs.

(b)(1) The master of a vessel of the United States required to report to the System shall report to the owner, charterer, managing operator, or agent at least once every 48 hours.

(2) A master violating this subsection is liable to the Government for a civil penalty of not more than $1,000 for each day during which the violation occurs.

(c) The Secretary may prescribe regulations to carry out this section.

ALTERNATIVE COMPLIANCE

The alternative compliance procedures for the International Rules and the Inland Rules are the same, although they appear both in the International Rules section of the Code of Federal Regulations (33 CFR Part 81) and in the Inland Rules section (33 CFR Part 89).
SEC
1. Definitions. 4. Certificate of Alternative Compliance: Contents.
2. General. 5. Certificate of Alternative Compliance: Termination.
3. Application for a Certificate 6. Record of certification of vessels of special of Alternative Compliance. construction or purpose.

1. Definitions.

As used in this part:

"72 COLREGS" refers to the International Regulations for Preventing Collisions at Sea, 1972, done at London, October 20, 1972, as rectified by the Proces-Verbal of December 1, 1973, as amended.

"Inland Rules" refers to the Inland Navigation Rules contained in the Inland Navigational Rules Act of 1980 (Pub. L. 96-591) and the technical annexes established under that Act. "A vessel of special construction or purpose" means a vessel designed or modified to perform a special function and whose arrangement is thereby made relatively inflexible. "Interference with the special function of the vessel" occurs when installation or use of lights, shapes, or sound-signaling appliances under the 72 COLREGS/Inland Rules prevents or significantly hinders the operation in which the vessel is usually engaged.

2. General.

Vessels of special construction or purpose which cannot fully comply with the light, shape, and sound signal provisions of the 72 COLREGS/Inland Rules without interfering with their special function may instead meet alternative requirements. The Chief of the Marine Safety Division in each Coast Guard District Office makes this determination and requires that alternative compliance be as close as possible with the 72 COLREGS/Inland Rules. These regulations set out the procedure by which a vessel may be certified for alternative compliance.

3. Application for a Certificate of Alternative Compliance.

(a) The owner, builder, operator, or agent of a vessel of special construction or purpose who believes the vessel cannot fully comply with the 72 COLREGS/Inland Rules light, shape, or sound signal provisions without interference with its special function may apply for a determination that alternative compliance is justified. The application must be in writing, submitted to the Chief of the Marine Safety

Division of the Coast Guard District in which the vessel is being built or operated, and include the following information:

(1) The name, address, and telephone number of the applicant.

(2) The identification of the vessel by its:
  (i) Official number;
  (ii) Shipyard hull number;
  (iii) Hull identification number; or
  (iv) State number, if the vessel does not have an official number or hull identification number.

(3) Vessel name and home port, if known.

(4) A description of the vessel's area of operation.

(5) A description of the provision for which the Certificate of Alternative Compliance is sought, including:
  (i) The 72 COLREGS/Inland Rules Rule or Annex section number for which the Certificate of Alternative Compliance is sought;
  (ii) A description of the special function of the vessel that would be interfered with by full compliance with the provision of that Rule or
    Annex section; and
  (iii) A statement of how full compliance would interfere with the special function of the vessel.

(6) A description of the alternative installation that is in closest possible compliance with the applicable 72 COLREGS/Inland Rules Rule or Annex section.

(7) A copy of the vessel's plans or an accurate scale drawing that clearly shows—
  (i) The required installation of the equipment under the 72 COLREGS/Inland Rules,
  (ii) The proposed installation of the equipment for which certification is being sought, and
  (iii) Any obstructions that may interfere with the equipment when installed in:

(A) The required location; and

(B) The proposed location.

(b) The Coast Guard may request from the applicant additional information concerning the application.

4. Certificate of Alternative Compliance: Contents.

The Chief of the Marine Safety Division issues the Certificate of Alternative Compliance to the vessel based on a determination that it cannot comply fully with 72 COLREGS/Inland Rules light, shape, and sound signal provisions without interference with its special function. This Certificate includes:

(a) Identification of the vessel as supplied in the application;

(b) The provision of the 72 COLREGS/Inland Rules for which the Certificate authorizes alternative compliance;

(c) A certification that the vessel is unable to comply fully with the 72 COLREGS/Inland Rules light, shape, and sound signal requirements without interference with its special function;

(d) A statement of why full compliance would interfere with the special function of the vessel;

(e) The required alternative installation;

(f) A statement that the required alternative installation is in the closest possible compliance with the 72 COLREGS/Inland Rules without interfering with the special function of the vessel;

(g) The date of issuance;

(h) A statement that the Certificate of Alternative Compliance terminates when the vessel ceases to be usually engaged in the operation for which the certificate is issued.

5. Certificate of Alternative Compliance: Termination.
The Certificate of Alternative Compliance terminates if the information supplied under 3.(a) or the Certificate issued under 4 is no longer applicable to the vessel.

6. Record of certification of vessels of special construction or purpose.

(a) Copies of Certificates of Alternative Compliance and documentation concerning Coast Guard vessels are available for inspection at the offices of Assistant Commandant for Marine Safety and Environmental Protection, U.S. Coast Guard Headquarters, 2100 Second Street, S.W., Washington, D.C. 20593-0001.

(b) The owner or operator of a vessel issued a certificate shall ensure that the vessel does not operate unless the Certificate of Alternative Compliance or a certified copy of that certificate is on board the vessel and available for inspection by Coast Guard personnel.

WATERS SPECIFIED BY THE SECRETARY

33 CFR §89.25 Waters upon which Inland Rules 9(a)(ii), 14(d), and 15(b) apply.

Inland Rules 9(a)(ii), 14(d), and 15(b) apply on the Great Lakes, the Western Rivers, and the following specified waters:

(a) Tennessee-Tombigbee Waterway;

(b) Tombigbee River;

(c) Black Warrior River;

(d) Alabama River;

(e) Coosa River;

(f) Mobile River above the Cochrane Bridge at St Louis Point;

(g) Flint River;

(h) Chattahoochee River, and

(i) The Apalachicola River above its confluence with the Jackson River.

33 CFR §89.27 Waters upon which Inland Rule 24(i) applies.

(a) Inland Rule 24(i) applies on the Western Rivers and the specified waters listed in §89.25 (a) through (i).

(b) Inland Rule 24(i) applies on the Gulf Intracoastal Waterway from St. Marks, Florida, to the Rio Grande, Texas, including the Morgan City-Port Allen Alternate Route and the Galveston-Freeport Cutoff, except that a power-driven vessel pushing ahead or towing alongside shall exhibit the lights required by Inland Rule 24(c), while transiting within the following areas:

(1) St. Andrews Bay from the Hathaway Fixed Bridge at Mile 284.6 East of Harvey Locks

(EHL) to the DuPont Fixed Bridge at Mile 295.4 EHL.

(2) Pensacola Bay, Santa Rosa Sound and Big Lagoon from the Light "10" off of Trout

Point at Mile 176.9 EHL to the Pensacola Fixed Bridge at Mile 189.1 EHL

(3) Mobile Bay and Bon Secour Bay from the Dauphin Island Causeway Fixed Bridge at

Mile 127.7 EHL to Little Point Clear at Mile 140 EHL.

(4) Mississippi Sound from Grand Island Waterway Light "1" at Mile 53.8 EHL to Light

"40" off the West Point of Dauphin Island at Mile 118.7 EHL

(5) The Mississippi River at New Orleans, Mississippi River-Gulf Outlet Canal and the

Inner Harbor Navigation Canal from the junction of the Harvey Canal and the Algiers

Alternate Route at Mile 6.5 West of Harvey Locks (WHL) to the Michoud Canal at Mile

18 EHL.

(6) The Calcasieu River from the Calcasieu Lock at Mile 238.6 WHL to the Ellender Lift

    Bridge at Mile 243.6 WHL.

(7) The Sabine Neches Canal from Mile 262.5 WHL to Mile 291.5 WHL.

(8) Bolivar Roads from the Bolivar Assembling Basin at Mile 346 WHL to the Galveston

    Causeway Bridge at Mile 357.3 WHL.

(9) Freeport Harbor from Surfside Beach Fixed Bridge at Mile 393.8 WHL to the Bryan

    Beach Pontoon Bridge at Mile 397.6 WHL.

(10) Matagorda Ship Channel area of Matagorda Bay from Range "K" Front Light at Mile

    468.7 WHL to the Port O'Connor Jetty at Mile 472.2 WHL.

(11) Corpus Christi Bay from Redfish Bay Day Beacon "55" at Mile 537.4 WHL when in

    the Gulf Intracoastal Waterway main route or from the north end of Lydia Ann Island

    Mile 531.1A when in the Gulf Intracoastal Waterway Alternate Route to Corpus Christl

    Bay LT 76 at Mile 543.7 WHL.

(12) Port Isabel and Brownsville Ship Channel south of the Padre Island Causeway Fixed

    Bridge at Mile 665.1 WHL.

VESSEL BRIDGE-TO-BRIDGE RADIOTELEPHONE REGULATIONS

33 CFR 26

The Vessel Bridge-to-Bridge Radiotelephone Act is applicable on navigable waters of the United States inside the boundary lines established in 46 CFR 7. In all cases, the Act applies on waters subject to the Inland Rules. The Act applies out to the three mile limit. In no instance does the Act apply beyond the three mile limit.

26.01 Purpose.

26.02 Definitions. failure of radiotelephone.

26.03 Radiotelephone required.

26.04 Use of the designated frequency.

26.05 Use of radiotelephone.

26.06 Maintenance of radiotelephone;

26.07 Communications.

26.08 Exemption procedures.

26.09 List of exemptions.

§ 26.01 Purpose.

(a) The purpose of this part is to implement the provisions of the

Vessel Bridge-to-Bridge Radiotelephone Act. This part:

(1) Requires the use of the vessel bridge-to-bridge radiotelephone;

(2) Provides the Coast Guard's interpretation of the meaning of important terms in the Act;

(3) Prescribes the procedures for applying for an exemption from the Act and the regulations issued under the Act and a listing of exemptions.

(b) Nothing in this part relieves any person from the obligation of complying with the rules of the road and the applicable pilot rules.

§ 26.02 Definitions.

For the purpose of this part and interpreting the Act:

"Secretary" means the Secretary of the Department in which the Coast Guard is operating;

"Act" means the "Vessel Bridge-to-Bridge Radiotelephone Act", 33 U.S.C. sections 1201–1208;

"Length" is measured from end to end over the deck excluding sheer;

"Power-driven vessel" means any vessel propelled by machinery;

"Towing vessel means any commercial vessel engaged in towing another vessel astern, alongside, or by pushing ahead;

"Vessel Traffic Services (VTS)" means a service implemented under Part 161 of this chapter by the United States Coast Guard designed to improve the safety and efficiency of vessel traffic and to protect the environment.

The VTS has the capability to interact with marine traffic and respond to traffic situations developing in the VTS area; and "Vessel Traffic Service Area or VTS Area" means the geographical area encompassing a specific VTS area of service as described in Part 161 of this chapter. This area of service may be subdivided into sectors for the purpose of allocating responsibility to individual Vessel Traffic Centers or to identify different operating requirements.

Note: Although regulatory jurisdiction is limited to the navigable waters of the United States, certain vessels will be encouraged or may be required, as a condition of port entry, to report beyond this area to facilitate traffic management within the VTS area.

§ 26.03 Radiotelephone required.

(a) Unless an exemption is granted under §26.09 and except as provided in paragraph (a) (4) of this section, this part applies to:

(1) Every power-driven vessel of 20 meters or over in length while navigating;

(2) Every vessel of 100 gross tons and upward carrying one or more passengers for hire while navigating;

(3) Every towing vessel of 26 feet or over in length while navigating; and

(4) Every dredge and floating plant engaged in or near a channel

or fairway in operations likely to restrict or affect navigation of other vessels except for an unmanned or intermittently manned floating plant under the control of a dredge.

(b) Every vessel, dredge, or floating plant described in paragraph

(a) of this section must have a radiotelephone on board capable of operation from its navigational bridge, or in the case of a dredge, from its main control station, and capable of transmitting and receiving on the frequency or frequencies within the 156-162 Mega-Hertz band using the classes of emissions designated by the Federal Communications Commission for the exchange of navigational information.

(c) The radiotelephone required by paragraph (b) of this section must be carried on board the described vessels, dredges, and floating plants upon the navigable waters of the United States.

(d) The radiotelephone required by paragraph (b) of this section must be capable of transmitting and receiving on VHF FM channel 22A (157.1 MHz).

(e) While transiting any of the following waters, each vessel described in paragraph (a) of this section also must have on board a radiotelephone capable of transmitting and receiving on VHF FM channel 67 (156.375 MHz):

(1) The lower Mississippi River from the territorial sea boundary, and within either the Southwest Pass safety fairway or the South Pass safety fairway specified in 33 CFR 166.200, to mile 242.4 AHP (Above Head of Passes) near Baton Rouge;

(2) The Mississippi River-Gulf Outlet from the territorial sea boundary, and within the Mississippi River-Gulf Outlet Safety Fairway specified in 33 CFR 166.200, to that channel's junction with the Inner Harbor Navigation Canal; and

(3) The full length of the Inner Harbor Navigation Canal from its junction with the Mississippi River to that canal's entry to Lake Pontchartrain at the New Seabrook vehicular bridge.

(f) In addition to the radiotelephone required by paragraph (b) of this section, each vessel described in paragraph (a) of this section while transiting any waters within a Vessel Traffic Service Area, must have on board a radiotelephone capable of transmitting and receiving on the VTS designated frequency in Table 26.03(f) (VTS Call Signs, Designated Frequencies, and Monitoring Areas).

Note: A single VHF FM radio capable of scanning or sequential monitoring (often referred to as "dual watch" capability) will not meet the requirements for two radios.

§ 26.04 Use of the designated frequency.

(a) No person may use the frequency designated by the Federal

Communications Commission under section 8 of the Act, 33 U.S.C. 1207(a), to transmit any information other than information necessary for the safe navigation of vessels or necessary tests.

(b) Each person who is required to maintain a listening watch under section 5 of the Act shall, when necessary, transmit and confirm, on the designated frequency, the intentions of his vessel and any other information necessary for the safe navigation of vessels.

(c) Nothing in these regulations may be construed as prohibiting the use of the designated frequency to communicate with shore stations to obtain or furnish information necessary for the safe navigation of vessels.

(d) On the navigable waters of the United States, channel 13 (156.65 MHz) is the designated frequency required to be monitored in accordance with §26.05(a) except that in the area prescribed in §26.03(e), channel 67 (156.375 MHz) is an additional frequency.

(e) On those navigable waters of the United States within a VTS area, the designated VTS frequency is the designated frequency required to be monitored in accordance with §26.05.

Note: As stated in 47 CFR 80.148(b), a VHF watch on Channel 16 (156.800Mhz) is not required on vessels subject to the Vessel Bridge-to-Bridge Radiotelephone Act and participating in a Vessel Traffic Service (VTS) system when the watch is maintained on both the vessel bridge-to-bridge frequency and a designated VTS frequency.

§ 26.05 Use of Radiotelephone.

Section 5 of the Act states that the radiotelephone required by this Act is for the exclusive use of the master or person in charge of the vessel, or the person designated by the master or person in charge to pilot or direct the movement of the vessel, who shall maintain a listening watch on the designated frequency. Nothing herein shall be interpreted as precluding the use of portable radiotelephone equipment to satisfy the requirements of this Act.

§ 26.06 Maintenance of radiotelephone; failure of radiotelephone.

Section 6 of the Act states that whenever radiotelephone capability is required by this Act, a vessel's radiotelephone equipment shall be maintained in effective operating condition. If the radiotelephone equipment carried aboard a vessel ceases to operate, the master shall exercise due diligence to restore it or cause it to be restored to effective operating condition at the earliest practicable time. The failure of a vessel's radiotelephone equipment shall not, in itself, constitute a violation of this Act, nor shall it obligate the master of any vessel to moor or anchor his vessel; however, the loss of radiotelephone capability shall be given consideration in the navigation of the vessel.

§ 26.07 Communications.

No person may use the services of, and no person may serve as, a person required to maintain a listening watch under section 5 of the Act, 33 U.S.C. 1204, unless the person can communicate in the English language.

§ 26.08 Exemption procedures.

(a) The Commandant has redelegated to the Assistant Commandant for Marine Safety and Environmental Protection, U.S. Coast Guard Headquarters, with the reservation that this authority shall not be further redelegated, the authority to grant exemptions from provisions of the Vessel Bridge-to-Bridge Radiotelephone Act and this part.

(b) Any person may petition for an exemption from any provision of the Act or this part;

(c) Each petition must be submitted in writing to U.S. Coast Guard, Marine Safety and Environmental Protection, 2100 Second Street, S.W., Washington, D.C. 20593-0001, and must state:

(1) The provisions of the Act or this part from which an exemption is requested; and

(2) The reasons why marine navigation will not be adversely affected if the exemption is granted and if the exemption relates to a local communication system how that system would fully comply with the intent of the concept of the Act but would not conform in detail if the exemption is granted.

§ 26.09 List of Exemptions.

(a) All vessels navigating on those waters governed by the navigation rules for the Great Lakes and their connecting and tributary waters (33 U.S.C. 241 et seq.) are exempt from the requirements of the Vessel Bridge-to-Bridge Radiotelephone Act and this part until May 6, 1975.

(b) Each vessel navigating on the Great Lakes as defined in the Inland Navigation Rules Act of 1980 (33 U.S.C. 2001 et seq.) and to which the Vessel Bridge-to-Bridge Radiotelephone Act (33 U.S.C. 1201-1208) applies is exempt from the requirements in 33 U.S.C. 1203, 1204, and 1205 and the regulations under §§26.03, 26.04, 26.05, 26.06, and 26.07. Each of these vessels and each person to whom 33 U.S.C. 1208(a) applies must comply with Articles VII, X, XI, XII, XIII, XV, and XVI and Technical Regulations 1-9 of "The Agreement Between the United States of America and Canada for Promotion of Safety on the Great Lakes by Means of Radio, 1973."

WHERE AND HOW TO CONTACT A VTS

For more information about each specific VTS, please visit their website or read their User Manual.

New York   Houston   Berwick Bay
St. Mary's River   San Francisco   Puget Sound
Prince William Sound Louisville   Notes

Notes 1 and 2, at the end of this section, apply to all VTS ports. You may address questions concerning VTS to fldr-g-mwv@comdt.usc.mil.

New York[3]: "New York Traffic"[4]
Channel Designation: Ch 11 (156.550 MHz)
                        Ch 14 (156.700 MHz)
Monitoring Area: The navigable waters of the Lower New York Harbor bounded on the east by a line drawn from Norton Point to Breezy Point; on the south by a line connecting the entrance buoys at the Ambrose Channel, Swash Channel and Sandy Hook Channel to Sandy Hook Point; and on the southeast including the waters of the Sandy Hook Bay south to a line drawn at latitude 40° 25' N.; then west into waters of the Raritan Bay to the Raritan River Rail Road Bridge; and then north including the waters of the Arthur Kill and Newark Bay to the Lehigh Valley Draw Bridge at latitude 40° 41.95' N.; and then east including the waters of the Kill Van Kull and Upper New York Bay north to a line drawn east-west from the Holland Tunnel Ventilator Shaft at latitude 40° 43.7' N.; longitude 74° 01.6' W. in the Hudson River; and continuing east including the waters of the East River to the Throgs Neck Bridge, excluding the Harlem River.
Channel Designation: Ch 12 (156.600 MHz)
Monitoring Area: Each vessel at anchor within the above areas.

Houston[3]: "Houston Traffic" (The navigable waters north of 29° N., west of 94° 20' W., south of 29° 49' N., and east of 95° 20' W.:
Channel Designation: Ch 11 (156.550 MHz)
Monitoring Area: The navigable waters north of a line extending due west from the southern most end of Exxon Dock #1 (29° 43.37' N., 95° 01.27' W.).
Channel Designation: Ch 12 (156.600 MHz)
Monitoring Area: The navigable waters north of a line extending due west from the southern most end of Exxon Dock #1 (29° 43.37' N., 95° 01.27' W.).

Berwick Bay: "Berwick Traffic"
Channel Designation: Ch 11 (156.550 MHz)
Monitoring Area: The navigable waters south of 29° 45' N., west of 91° 10'
W., north of 29° 37' N., and east of 91° 18' W.

St. Marys River: "Soo Control"
Channel Designation: Ch 11 (156.550 MHz)
                         Ch 12 (156.600 MHz)
Monitoring Area: The navigable waters of the St. Marys River between 45°
57' N. (De Tour Reef Light) and 46° 38.7' N. (lle Parisienne Light), except
the St. Marys Falls Canal and those navigable waters east of a line from 46°
04.16'N. and 46° 01.57' N. (La Pointe to Sims Point in Patagannissing Bay
and Worsley Bay).

San Francisco[3]:
"San Francisco Offshore Vessel Movement Reporting Service"
Channel Designation: Ch 12 (156.600 MHz)
Monitoring Area: The waters within a 38 nautical mile radius of Mount
Tamalpais (37° 55.8' N.,   122° 34.6' W.) excluding the San Francisco
Offshore Precautionary Area.
"San Francisco Traffic"
Channel Designation: Ch 14 (156.700 MHz)
Monitoring Area: The waters of the San Francisco Offshore Precautionary
Area eastward to San Francisco Bay including its tributaries extending to the
ports of Stockton, Sacramento and Redwood Clty.

Puget Sound[5]:
"Seattle Traffic"[6]
Channel Designation: Ch 14 (156.700 MHz)
Monitoring Area: The navigable waters of Puget Sound, Hood Canal and ad-
jacent waters south of a line connecting Marrowstone Point and Lagoon Point
in Admiralty inlet and south of a line drawn due east from the southernmost
tip of Possession Point on Whidbey Island to the shoreline.
Channel Designation: Ch 5A (156.250 MHz)
Monitoring Area: The navigable waters of the Strait of Juan de Fuca east of
124° 40' W. excluding the waters in the central portion of the Strait of Juan
de Fuca north and east of Race Rocks; the navigable waters of the Strait of
Georgia east of 122° 52' W.; the San Juan Island Archipelago, Rosario Strait,
Bellingham Bay; Admiralty inlet north of a line connecting Marrowstone
Point and Lagoon Point and all waters east of Whidbey Island north of a line
drawn due east from the southernmost tip of Possession Point on Whidbey
Island to the shoreline.

"Tofino Traffic"[7]
Channel Designation: Ch 74 (156.725 MHz)
Monitoring Area: The waters west of 124° 40' W. within 50 nautical miles of the coast of Vancouver Island including the waters north of 48° N ., and east of 127° W.

"Vancouver Traffic"
Channel Designation: Ch 11 (156.550 MHz)
Monitoring Area: The navigable waters of the Strait of Georgia west of 122° 52' W., the navigable waters of the central Strait of Juan de Fuca north and east of Race Rocks, Including the Gulf Island Archipelago, Boundary Pass and Haro Strait.

Prince William Sound[8]: "Valdez Traffic"
Channel Designation: Ch 13 (156.650 MHz)
Monitoring Area: The navigable waters south of 61° 05' N., east of 147° 20' W., north of 60° N., and west of 146° 30' W.; and, all navigable waters in Port Valdez.

Louisville[8]: "Louisville Traffic"
Channel Designation: Ch 13 (156.650 MHz)
Monitoring Area: The navigable waters of the Ohio River between McAlpine Locks (Mile 606) and Twelve Mile Island (Mile 593), only when the McAlpine upper pool gauge is at approximately 13.0 feet or above.

Notes:
1. VTS regulations are denoted in 33 CFR Part 161. All geographic coordinates (latitude and longitude) are expressed in North American Datum of 1983 (NAD 83).

2. In the event of a communication failure either by the vessel traffic center or the vessel or radio congestion on a designated VTS frequency, communications may be established on an alternate VTS frequency. The bridge-to-bridge navigational frequency 156.650 MHz (Channel 13), is monitored in each VTS area; and it may be used as an alternate frequency, however, only to the extent that doing so provides a level of safety beyond that provided by other means.

3. Designated frequency monitoring is required within U.S. navigable waters. In areas which are outside the U.S. navigable waters, designated frequency monitoring is voluntary. However, prospective VTS Users are encouraged to monitor the designated frequency.

4. VMRS participants shall make their initial report (Sail Plan) to New York Traffic on Channel 11 (156.550 MHz). All other reports, including the Final Report, shall be made on Channel 14 (156.700 MHz.). VMRS and other VTS Users shall monitor Channel 14 (156.700 MHz) while transiting the VTS

area. New York Traffic may direct a vessel to monitor and report on either primary frequency depending on traffic density, weather conditions, or other safety factors. This does not require a vessel to monitor both primary frequencies.

5. A Cooperative Vessel Traffic Service was established by the United States and Canada within adjoining waters. The appropriate vessel traffic center administers the rules issued by both nations; however, it will enforce only its own set of rules within its jurisdiction.

6. Seattle Traffic may direct a vessel to monitor the other primary VTS frequency 156.250 MHz or 156.700 MHz (Channel 5A or 14) depending on traffic density, weather conditions, or other safety factors, rather than strictly adhering to the designated frequency required for each monitoring area as defined above. This does not require a vessel to monitor both primary frequencies.

7. A portion of Tofino Sector's monitoring area extends beyond the defined CVTS area. Designated frequency monitoring is voluntary in these portions outside of VTS jurisdiction, however, prospective VTS Users are encouraged to monitor the designated frequency.

8. The bridge-to-bridge navigational frequency, 156.650 MHz (Channel 13), is used in these VTSs because the level of radiotelephone transmissions does not warrant a designated VTS frequency. The listening watch required by 26.05 of this chapter is not limited to the monitoring area.

LEGAL CITATIONS

The Rules, as presented in this book, are not the legal basis upon which any action can be taken. The actual laws and regulations governing maritime activity are, in fact, referenced here. –The Editors

72 COLREGS

International Navigational Rules	Public Law 95-75;
Act of 1977	91 Stat. 308;
33 U.S.C. 1601-1608	
COLREGS Demarcation Lines	33 CFR 80
72 COLREGS: Implementing Rules	33 CFR 81
72 COLREGS: Interpretative Rules	33 CFR 82
Amendments to 72 COLREGS effective	48 FR 28634
June 1, 1983	

INLAND RULES

Inland Navigational Rules Act of 1980	Public Law 96-591;
94 Stat. 3415;	
33 U.S.C. 2001-2038,	

Annex l: Positioning and Technical   33 CFR 84
Details of Lights and Shapes
Annex Il: Additional Signals for Fishing   33 CFR 85
in Close Proximity
Annex lll: Technical Details of Sound   33 CFR 86
Signal Appliances
Annex IV: Distress Signals   33 CFR 87
Annex V: Pilot Rules   33 CFR 88
Inland Navigation Rules: Implementing   33 CFR 89
Rules
Inland Navigation Rules: Interpretative   33 CFR 90
Rules

VESSEL BRIDGE-TO-BRIDGE RADIOTELEPHONE

Vessel Bridge-to-Bridge Radiotelephone   Public Law 92-63;
Act 33 U.S.C. 1201-1208   85 Stat.164;
Vessel Bridge-to-Bridge Radiotelephone   33 CFR 26
Regulations (Coast Guard regulations)
Radiotelephone Stations Provided for 47
CFR 80.1001 -80.1023
Compliance With the Vessel Bridge-to
Bridge Radiotelephone Act (Federal
Communications Commission regulations)
Other FCC regulations pertaining to vessel
bridge-to-bridge radiotelephone
communications are contained in various
sections of 47 CFR 80.
Boundary Lines   46 CFR 7

NOTES

NOTES

NOTES

NOTES

NOTES

NOTES

NOTES

NOTES

NOTES

NOTES

CONVERSION TABLE

Conversion of Metric to U.S. Customary/Imperial Units

Metric Measure	U.S. Customary/ Imperial Measure (Approx.)
1000 Meters (M)	3280.8 ft.
500 M	1640.4 ft.
200 M	656.2 ft.
150 M	492.1 ft.
100 M	328.1 ft.
75 M	246.1 ft.
60 M	196.8 ft.
50 M	164.0 ft.
25 M	82.0 ft.
20 M	65.6 ft.
12 M	39.4 ft.
10 M	32.8 ft.
8 M	26.2 ft.
7 M	23.0 ft.
6 M	19.7 ft.
5 M	16.4 ft.
4.5 M	14.8 ft.
4.0 M	13.1 ft.
3.5 M	11.5 ft.
2.5 M	8.2 ft.
2.0 M	6.6 ft.
1.5 M	4.9 ft.
1 M	3.3 ft.
.9 M	35.4 in.
.6M	23.6 in.
.5 M	19.7 in.
300 Millimeters (mm)	11.8 in.
200 mm	7.9 in.